QUICK PREP *Paleo*

Simple Whole-Food Meals *with* 5 to 15 Minutes of Hands-On Time

Mary Smith

**Creator of
Mary's Whole Life**

PAGE STREET
PUBLISHING CO.

PAGE STREET
PUBLISHING CO.

Copyright © 2020 Mary Smith

First published in 2020 by
Page Street Publishing Co.
27 Congress Street, Suite 105
Salem, MA 01970
www.pagestreetpublishing.com

Distributed by Macmillan, sales in Canada by The Canadian Manda Group.

24 23 22 21 20   1 2 3 4 5

ISBN-13: 978-1-64567-108-4
ISBN-10: 1-64567-108-9

Library of Congress Control Number: 2019957308

Cover and book design by Rosie Stewart for Page Street Publishing Co.
Photography by Mary Smith

Printed and bound in China

Dedication

To Annabel, Finn and Liam—being your mommy is both an honor and a privilege.

And to my husband, Bryan, for always believing in me, for being the ultimate taste-tester and for never hesitating to stop at the grocery store on your way home from work. I love you.

Table of Contents

Introduction

Ever since I was a little girl, I have always loved food. When I was diagnosed with celiac disease in 2016, I had to figure out how to continue eating (and cooking) delicious food using different ingredients. I could no longer have gluten, and I realized that I felt better if I didn't eat dairy. When I discovered the Paleo diet, I started to feel better than I had in years. I began to experiment in the kitchen and saw how fun it was to try to recreate some of my favorite dishes using real-food ingredients. This is when my blog, Mary's Whole Life, was born. It's been so exciting helping others realize that switching to a Paleo lifestyle doesn't have to be hard, complicated or time-consuming, and eating this way can still be delicious, easy and fun!

As a busy working mom of three children, I don't have a ton of time to spend in the kitchen, and I know many of you don't either. This is why I am so excited about the concept of this book. Quick prep = recipes that can all be chopped, diced, mixed and sautéed within 5 to 15 minutes before popping them into the oven, pressing start or covering them and walking away. This means you will have more time to do other things you love!

I approached the development of the recipes for this book with efficiency in mind. I want to help you make the best use of your time! A key tip for saving time in the kitchen is chopping veggies or gathering ingredients while your meat is browning or while your skillet or pot is heating up. The prep times listed in the recipes are based on multitasking and working efficiently in this way. If you'd like to cut the prep times down even more, some additional tips include buying pre-chopped and pre-spiralized vegetables, which can be found in most grocery stores. For instance, I always use pre-minced garlic. I also recommend chopping and/or prepping different meal components ahead of time when you can. For example, for the Meat Lovers' Pizza Spaghetti Squash Casserole (page 125), you can save time by making the spaghetti squash ahead of time and storing it in the refrigerator until you are ready to assemble the casserole.

Since comfort food is simply the best, many of the recipes in this book are recreations of childhood favorites using healthier ingredients and simpler cooking methods. Cashews, for example, are incredible to use in recipes because when blended, they can create decadent, creamy sauces that taste very similar to dairy. It's remarkable how dishes like Jalapeño Tuna Noodle Casserole (page 130), "Cheese"-Burger Casserole (page 129) and Slow Cooker Smothered Pork Chops (page 50) all taste just like the versions you grew up loving, but are so much better for you!

Whether you are switching to a Paleo diet for the first time or have been living this lifestyle for some time now, the recipes in this book will keep things easy and exciting. Eliminating gluten, dairy, grains, legumes and refined sugar has been known to improve sleep, decrease gastro-intestinal issues, decrease inflammation and improve mental clarity. I personally experienced all of these benefits after switching my diet, which is why I am so passionate about creating and sharing these types of recipes with others.

There is something for everyone in this book, whether you are trying to eat low carb, have a nut allergy or can't eat eggs. I tried to include ways to alter the recipes to suit different needs, because I know firsthand how challenging it can be to have an allergy or dietary restriction. I've also included tips on how to save even more time in the kitchen where relevant. You'll also find a variety of cooking methods—sheet-pan meals, slow cooker and Instant Pot® dishes, one-pot meals and casseroles, to name a few.

It can be hard to balance it all, but my hope is that with this book, cooking will become one less thing for you to stress out about. I hope you'll feel empowered to whip up delicious, real-food, family-friendly meals without having to spend hours in the kitchen. These recipes are simple enough for everyone to make, even if you're intimidated by the idea of cooking or feel like you just don't have the time. If I can do it, so can you!

Cheers,

Mary Smith

A Note on the Recipes

Rather than listing the prep and cook times for each recipe, I have broken it down by Hands-On Time and Hands-Off Time. This will help you determine which recipes will fit into your schedule on busy nights, and which ones would be better options for days when you have a little more time. The Hands-On Times listed are based on an experienced cook working quickly. Please keep this in mind as you are prepping.

Simple
Sheet-Pan Dinners

Sheet-pan dinners are one of my favorite things to make, especially on busy weeknights. It's so nice to simply toss your ingredients together and let the oven do the work. The recipes in this chapter are not only quick to prep, but all of the ingredients get cooked on one or two baking sheets at the same time. This makes for super-easy cleanup, which is always a win in my book! Sheet-pan dinners are an easy method to use when it comes to Paleo cooking, since meats, vegetables and seafood roast up wonderfully in the oven.

I like to include a good marinade or sauce with my sheet-pan recipes to keep them from becoming too dry. One of my personal favorites (and the number-one recipe on my website) is the Sausage, Potatoes and Broccoli Sheet-Pan Supper (page 17). Everything gets tossed in a delicious marinade prior to baking, which gives an otherwise simple meal a standout flavor profile. My family has been known to eat it straight off the pan while standing at the stove!

The other wonderful thing about sheet-pan dinners is that they often yield a lot of leftovers. This makes them a great option for meal prepping and saving yourself a lot of time in the kitchen. I'll often make one of these recipes on a Sunday night so that we start the week off with lunches already prepared and ready to reheat.

Some of my other favorites in this chapter include Sheet-Pan Chicken Pad Thai (page 22), Harvest Sheet-Pan Chicken and Root Veggies (page 10) and Sheet-Pan Pineapple Shrimp Fajitas (page 29).

Harvest Sheet-Pan Chicken and Root Veggies

Egg Free, Nut Free

While this sheet-pan meal is perfect to make during any season, it definitely reminds me of fall! It is filled with savory flavors from the herbs and a bit of sweet and tart from the cranberries. The potatoes, squash, cranberries and onions get cooked in the juices from the chicken, giving them the most incredible flavor. The best part . . . this is all cooked on one pan for an easy, stress-free meal with minimal cleanup!

Yield: *3–4 servings*
Hands-On Time: *10 minutes*
Hands-Off Time: *45 minutes*

1 medium sweet potato, scrubbed and cut into 1-inch (2.5-cm) cubes

4 cups (560 g) cubed butternut squash

1 medium onion, diced

½ cup (50 g) fresh or frozen cranberries

2 cloves garlic, minced

1 tbsp (15 ml) olive oil

1 tsp sea salt, divided

1 tbsp (15 ml) melted ghee

2 tsp (1 g) chopped fresh rosemary or ½ tsp dried

2 tsp (1 g) chopped fresh thyme or ½ tsp dried

1 tsp garlic powder

6 bone-in, skin-on chicken thighs (see Cooking Tip)

Preheat the oven to 425°F (220°C). Line a large rimmed baking sheet with parchment paper.

Add the sweet potato, butternut squash, onion, cranberries and garlic to the baking sheet. Drizzle with the olive oil and sprinkle with ½ teaspoon of the salt. Toss to combine. In a small bowl, mix together the ghee, rosemary, thyme, garlic powder and remaining salt until a paste forms. Place the chicken thighs on top of the veggies, skin side up. Use your fingers to spread some of the ghee and herb mixture onto each chicken thigh, making sure to coat them completely. Bake for 40 to 45 minutes, or until the internal temperature of the chicken reaches at least 170°F (77°C). For extra-crispy chicken, broil for 5 minutes!

Cooking Tip: *For crispier chicken, you can place the thighs on a metal baking rack on top of the potatoes, squash, onions and cranberries.*

Sheet-Pan Baja Fish Taco Bowls

Egg-Free Option, Low Carb, Nut Free

A good fish taco is my love language. In this recipe, the cod (or fish of choice) is seasoned and cooked alongside cauliflower rice on the same pan. One pan = fewer dishes, which is a win in my book! The garlic-lime aioli can be mixed up in less than 2 minutes and is the perfect creamy, tangy addition to these taco bowls. This recipe is totally customizable, but I like to serve mine on a bed of greens with avocado, red onion, cilantro, a squeeze of lime juice and copious amounts of aioli.

Yield: *3-4 servings*

Hands-On Time: *10 minutes*

Hands-Off Time: *20 minutes*

For the Fish

1 (16-oz [454-g]) bag frozen cauliflower rice (see Cooking Tips)

2 tbsp (30 ml) olive oil, divided

¾ tsp sea salt, divided

½ tsp chili powder

½ tsp cumin

½ tsp garlic powder

½ tsp paprika

½ tsp onion powder

¼ tsp black pepper

4 (6-8-oz [170-226-g]) cod fillets (or any white fish of choice, see Cooking Tips)

For the Garlic-Lime Aioli

½ cup (120 ml) mayonnaise (see Cooking Tips)

½ tbsp (8 ml) lime juice

1 clove garlic, minced

For Serving

Greens, fresh cilantro, limes, avocado and/or red onion, as needed

Preheat the oven to 400°F (200°C). Line a rimmed baking sheet with parchment paper for easy cleanup.

Place the cauliflower rice onto the pan, using a spatula to spread it out evenly. Drizzle with 1 tablespoon (15 ml) of the olive oil and ½ teaspoon of the salt. Toss to coat. Bake for 10 minutes.

Meanwhile, in a small bowl, combine the chili powder, cumin, garlic powder, paprika, onion powder, pepper and remaining salt. Place the cod fillets onto a plate and dry with a paper towel. Drizzle both sides with the remaining olive oil and use your hands to coat each fillet. Sprinkle an even amount of the seasoning mixture onto each fillet, then use your fingers to rub it in.

After the cauliflower rice has cooked for 10 minutes, remove it from the oven and push it to the sides of the pan to make room for the fillets. Add the fish to the pan and cook for 10 to 12 minutes, or until the fish flakes easily with a fork.

While the fish is cooking, make the garlic-lime aioli. In a small bowl, combine the mayonnaise, lime juice and garlic, and mix well. Store in the refrigerator until you're ready to serve it. Serve the cauliflower rice and fish in bowls with the garlic-lime aioli and desired toppings.

Cooking Tips: *I prefer to use frozen cauliflower rice rather than fresh. It has a really great texture.*

You can use any type of white fish for this recipe. The cooking time will depend on the thickness of the fish.

You can substitute vegan mayonnaise for the regular mayonnaise for an egg-free option.

Italian Turkey Meatloaf with Potatoes and Crispy Green Beans

Low-Carb Option, Nut-Free Option

Meatloaf is one of those staple meals that remind me of my childhood. It also happens to be delicious and quite easy to make. For this version, I use lean ground turkey, Italian spices and sugar-free marinara sauce to give it a twist from classic meatloaf. It gets baked on the same baking sheet as the potatoes and green beans, so you can have dinner ready in 1 hour, with minimal cleanup! I like to use a large 15 x 21-inch (38 x 53-cm) baking sheet for this recipe to ensure everything has enough space to crisp up without being too crowded. If you don't have a large baking sheet, simply cook the meatloaf on one pan and the potatoes and green beans on another.

Yield: *3-4 servings*
Hands-On Time: *15 minutes*
Hands-Off Time: *45 minutes*

For the Meatloaf

1⅓ lbs (605 g) lean ground turkey (see Cooking Tips)

½ small onion, diced fine

1 egg

¼ cup (60 ml) sugar-free marinara sauce (I like Rao's Homemade brand)

¼ cup (24 g) almond flour (see Cooking Tips)

1 tbsp (15 ml) coconut aminos

2 cloves garlic, minced

¼ cup (15 g) chopped fresh parsley

1 tsp Italian seasoning

½ tsp sea salt

¼ tsp black pepper

For the Vegetables

12 oz (340 g) green beans, ends chopped

1½ lbs (680 g) baby red potatoes, halved (see Cooking Tips)

1 tbsp (15 ml) olive oil

½ tsp sea salt

½ tsp Italian seasoning

Preheat the oven to 400°F (200°C). Line a large rimmed baking sheet with parchment paper.

To make the meatloaf, in a large bowl, add the turkey, onion, egg, marinara sauce, almond flour, coconut aminos, garlic, parsley, Italian seasoning, salt and pepper. Mix well using your hands. Place the mixture in the middle of the baking sheet. Form it into a loaf shape approximately 4 x 8 inches (10 x 20 cm).

To make the vegetables, in a large bowl, add the green beans, potatoes and olive oil and toss to coat. Spread the green beans and potatoes out evenly around the meatloaf. Sprinkle with the salt and Italian seasoning. Bake for 45 minutes, or until the internal temperature of the meatloaf is at least 170°F (77°C). Slice the meatloaf and serve alongside the potatoes and green beans.

Cooking Tips: *Some ground turkey is sold in 1⅓-pound (605-g) packages. If you cannot find this amount, 1 pound (454 g) will work with all of the same measurements of everything else.*

To make this nut free, substitute the almond flour with 1½ tablespoons (12 g) of coconut flour.

To make this low carb, omit the potatoes and add extra green beans or another vegetable of your choice.

Sausage, Potatoes and Broccoli Sheet-Pan Supper

Egg Free, Low-Carb Option, Nut Free

This has been the most popular recipe on my blog for the past 2 years, so I knew I just had to include it in this book! I love this sheet-pan meal because it is so easy to make, the leftovers make a great breakfast or lunch and it's just so delicious (and addicting . . . you've been warned!). The best part is that everything gets tossed in a delicious marinade before baking, so you don't have to worry about anything lacking flavor or drying out. Feel free to get creative and use any other vegetables that you want.

Yield: *3-4 servings*
Hands-On Time: *10 minutes*
Hands-Off Time: *30 minutes*

1 (12-oz [340-g]) package sugar-free sausage of choice (I like Aidells Chicken & Apple Sausage), cut into ½-inch (1.3-cm) pieces

12 oz (340 g) broccoli florets

6 medium-sized red potatoes, cut into 1- to 2-inch (2.5- to 5-cm) cubes (see Cooking Tip)

½ cup (120 ml) olive or avocado oil

¼ cup (60 ml) coconut aminos

2 tbsp (30 ml) Dijon mustard

1 tbsp (15 ml) hot sauce (I like Frank's RedHot)

2 cloves garlic, minced

1 tsp onion powder

1 tsp sea salt

½ tsp crushed red pepper flakes (more or less, depending on how spicy you like it)

Dairy-free ranch dressing (I like Tessamae's, optional)

Preheat the oven to 425°F (220°C). Line a rimmed 15 x 21-inch (38 x 53-cm) baking sheet with parchment paper or foil for easier cleanup, if desired. A smaller pan can be used but will yield less-crispy results.

Add the sausage and broccoli to a large bowl. Add the potatoes to a second large bowl. In a medium bowl, whisk the oil, coconut aminos, mustard, hot sauce, garlic, onion powder, salt and crushed red pepper flakes. Pour half over the potatoes and the rest over the broccoli and sausage. Mix each bowl well.

Pour the potatoes onto the baking sheet and roast for 20 minutes. Add the broccoli and sausage mixture and toss with the partially roasted potatoes. Roast for an additional 10 to 15 minutes, or until the broccoli is browned to your liking. Serve with ranch dressing, if desired.

Cooking Tip: *Omit the potatoes and swap in halved radishes for a lower-carb option.*

Almond-Crusted Cod with Broccoli

Egg Free, Low Carb

Nut-crusted fish is one of my favorite ways to eat seafood. This recipe uses a blend of almonds, fresh parsley, nutritional yeast (which gives it a "cheesy" flavor) and spices as the crust, which pairs beautifully with the roasted broccoli. I usually always have frozen wild-caught cod in my freezer so I can quickly thaw it for easy meals like this! The fish and the broccoli roast simultaneously, getting dinner on the table in less than 30 minutes. You can use pecans, macadamia nuts or any other type of nut you would like for the crust.

Yield: *3-4 servings*
Hands-On Time: *10 minutes*
Hands-Off Time: *15 minutes*

3 (6-oz [170-g]) cod fillets, thawed if previously frozen

⅔ cup (94 g) raw unsalted almonds (see Cooking Tip)

¼ cup (15 g) nutritional yeast

¼ cup (15 g) fresh parsley

2 tbsp (30 ml) olive oil, divided

½ tsp garlic powder

1 tsp sea salt, divided

1 tbsp (15 ml) melted ghee

12 oz (340 g) broccoli florets

1 tbsp (15 ml) lemon juice

Lemon slices, for serving

Preheat the oven to 400°F (200°C). Line a rimmed baking sheet with parchment paper. Pat the cod fillets with a paper towel to remove any excess moisture, and place them in the center of the baking sheet.

In a food processor or high-speed blender, add the almonds, nutritional yeast, parsley, 1 tablespoon (15 ml) of the olive oil, garlic powder and ½ teaspoon of the salt. Pulse a few times until all of the ingredients are crumbled and combined.

Brush the ghee onto each piece of cod. Top each piece with some of the almond crust, and use your fingers to press it down gently. You will have some left over, which you will use shortly!

In a large bowl, toss the broccoli with the remaining olive oil and salt. Use your fingers to massage the olive oil into the broccoli for maximum flavor. Add the broccoli to the baking sheet, covering the areas around the fish. Sprinkle any remaining almond crust onto the broccoli florets. Drizzle the lemon juice over the fish and the broccoli. Bake for 15 minutes, or until the cod flakes easily using a fork. Serve with an extra slice of lemon on top.

Cooking Tip: *If you do not have a high-speed blender like a Vitamix, I recommend soaking the almonds for at least 1 hour and then draining them before blending.*

Sheet-Pan Italian Sausage, Peppers and Eggplant

Egg Free, Nut Free

This one-pan meal combines two delightful Italian dishes: sausage and peppers and eggplant parmesan. Except there is no dairy or gluten involved! Coating the veggies in marinara and Italian spices before baking gives them the most incredible flavor. The sausage gets roasted right on top of the veggies, so there is minimal cleanup and only one pan involved. This could be served as is, on top of a salad, with cauliflower rice or with Garlic Cauliflower Mash (page 162).

Yield: *3-4 servings*

Hands-On Time: *10 minutes*

Hands-Off Time: *30 minutes*

1 green bell pepper, deseeded and sliced

1 red bell pepper, deseeded and sliced

1 small onion, sliced into thin strips

1 small eggplant, chopped into 1-inch (2.5-cm) cubes

2 cloves garlic, minced

1 tbsp (15 ml) olive oil

½ cup (120 ml) marinara sauce (I like Rao's Homemade brand)

1 tsp Italian seasoning

½ tsp sea salt

1 lb (454 g) sugar-free Italian sausage (approximately 5 links, see Cooking Tip)

Preheat the oven to 425°F (220°C). Line a rimmed baking sheet with parchment paper for easy cleanup.

In a large bowl, mix together the green bell pepper, red bell pepper, onion, eggplant, garlic, olive oil, marinara sauce, Italian seasoning and salt. Spread the mixture out evenly onto the baking sheet. Place the sausages on top. Bake for 30 minutes, or until the sausages are cooked through. Serve the sausages on top of a bed of the peppers, onion and eggplant.

Cooking Tip: *You can use any type of sausage for this recipe.*

Sheet-Pan Chicken Pad Thai

Egg-Free Option, Nut-Free Option, Vegan Option

Traditional pad thai is made with soy sauce, rice noodles and peanuts. We are replacing these with spaghetti squash, almond butter and cashews to keep it Paleo and gluten-free! This dish is a healthier version with all of the traditional flavors. This dish takes 15 minutes to prep for someone who is experienced in the kitchen and moving quickly. If you are working leisurely, it may take longer than that, but it is worth the effort!

Yield: *4 servings*
Hands-On Time: *15 minutes*
Hands-Off Time: *35 minutes*

For the Chicken and Veggies

1 large spaghetti squash

1½ lbs (680 g) chicken breasts, sliced thin

1 red bell pepper, deseeded and sliced

1 cup (110 g) julienne carrots

Pinch of sea salt

1 tbsp (15 ml) sesame or olive oil

Avocado or olive oil cooking spray

2 eggs, beaten (optional)

For the Sauce

½ cup (129 g) almond butter (see Cooking Tips)

½ cup (120 ml) full-fat coconut milk (stir well before measuring)

2 tbsp (30 ml) maple syrup

3 cloves garlic, minced

1 tbsp (5 g) ground ginger

1 tbsp (15 ml) rice vinegar

1 tbsp (15 ml) fish sauce

1 tbsp (15 ml) fresh lime juice

2 tbsp (30 ml) coconut aminos

½ tsp crushed red pepper flakes

For Garnishing

¼ cup (32 g) chopped cashews

¼ cup (4 g) chopped cilantro

Lime wedges

Preheat the oven to 400°F (200°C). Line two baking sheets with parchment paper.

To make the chicken and veggies, cut the spaghetti squash in half and scoop out the seeds. Place the halves cut side down on one of the baking sheets. Roast the squash for 35 minutes. In a large bowl, toss the chicken, bell pepper, carrots, salt and sesame oil. Spread everything out evenly on the second baking sheet. Add to the oven when the squash has 25 minutes of cooking time remaining.

To make the sauce, in a medium bowl, whisk together the almond butter, coconut milk, maple syrup, garlic, ginger, rice vinegar, fish sauce, lime juice, coconut aminos and crushed red pepper flakes. Set aside.

When the squash and chicken have 5 minutes left, make the scrambled eggs (if using). Heat a small skillet over medium heat, spray with the avocado or olive oil and scramble the eggs.

Scoop the spaghetti squash strands out of the cooked squash and add to the pan with the cooked chicken and bell pepper. Add the scrambled eggs (if using) and the sauce, and toss to combine. Serve topped with the chopped nuts, cilantro and a squeeze of lime juice.

Cooking Tips: *You can make the sauce and/or spaghetti squash up to 2 days ahead of time.*

Sunflower seed butter can be substituted for the almond butter for a nut-free recipe. Omit the cashews for garnishing.

To make this vegan, omit the chicken, eggs and fish sauce and add an extra red bell pepper and an extra teaspoon of coconut aminos.

Asian Salmon and Stir-Fry Veggies

Egg Free, Low-Carb Option, Nut Free

This sheet-pan salmon has a delicious, slightly sweet teriyaki glaze, tender crisp veggies and all of the flavors of a stir-fry without the effort! This is a perfect weeknight meal or a lovely way to entertain stress free if you're having guests over for dinner. To save time, I like to get a mixed pack of pre-cut stir-fry veggies.

Yield: *4 servings*
Hands-On Time: *15 minutes*
Hands-Off Time: *15 minutes*

½ cup (120 ml) coconut aminos

1 tbsp (15 ml) rice vinegar

2 tsp (10 ml) sesame oil

2 cloves garlic, minced

½ tsp fish sauce

1 tsp grated ginger

1 tbsp (15 ml) honey (see Cooking Tip)

2 tsp (5 g) arrowroot powder

2 tbsp (30 ml) water

1 red bell pepper, sliced

½ red onion, sliced

2 cups (182 g) broccoli florets

½ cup (62 g) sliced water chestnuts

4 (6-oz [170-g]) salmon fillets

2 tbsp (6 g) diced green onions (optional)

1 tbsp (9 g) sesame seeds (optional)

Preheat the oven to 400°F (200°C). Line a rimmed baking sheet with foil for easy cleanup.

To make the glaze, add the coconut aminos, rice vinegar, sesame oil, garlic, fish sauce, ginger and honey to a small saucepan. Bring it to a boil. In a small bowl, whisk the arrowroot powder and water to create a slurry, and add it to the pan. It will thicken almost immediately as you whisk. Set the glaze aside.

Add the bell pepper, onion, broccoli and water chestnuts to the baking sheet. Make some space for the salmon fillets and place them in the middle of the pan. Drizzle half of the glaze over the veggies, and brush the rest over the salmon fillets (top and sides). Reserve about 1 tablespoon (15 ml) of the glaze. Bake the fish and veggies for 10 minutes.

Remove the pan from the oven and brush each salmon fillet with the remaining glaze. Turn the oven to broil, and return the pan to the oven. Broil for 4 to 5 minutes, or until the veggies and salmon are nicely browned and the salmon flakes easily using a fork. Serve with green onions and sesame seeds, if desired.

Cooking Tip: *Omit the honey to make this recipe sugar free/low carb.*

Prosciutto, Chicken and Asparagus Bundles with Blistered Tomatoes

Egg Free, Low Carb, Nut Free

I love this meal for three main reasons: 1) It's all cooked on one pan, which always makes life easier, 2) It's simple yet fancy enough to serve at a dinner party and 3) It only uses a few simple ingredients. The saltiness from the prosciutto plus the balsamic vinegar create the perfect juicy chicken, tender asparagus and flavorful blistered tomatoes. You can serve this as is or over mashed potatoes, Garlic Cauliflower Mash (page 162) or on a salad.

Yield: *4 servings*
Hands-On Time: *10 minutes*
Hands-Off Time: *25 minutes*

2 large chicken breasts, cut in half lengthwise to create 4 thinner breasts

¼ tsp sea salt

1 tsp Italian seasoning

16 pieces asparagus

4 pieces prosciutto

1½ cups (224 g) cherry tomatoes

¼ cup (60 ml) olive oil

2 tbsp (30 ml) balsamic vinegar

Preheat the oven to 425°F (220°C). Line a baking sheet with parchment paper or aluminum foil for easy cleanup.

Lay the chicken breast halves on a cutting board and with a mallet pound to a ¼-inch (6-mm) thickness. Sprinkle the salt and Italian seasoning over both sides of the breast halves. Place 4 asparagus pieces inside each chicken breast piece and roll them up. Wrap 1 piece of prosciutto around each chicken roll-up, and secure everything with a toothpick. Place the chicken bundles onto the baking sheet. Place the tomatoes around the chicken bundles.

In a small bowl, whisk the olive oil and balsamic vinegar until combined. Spoon some of the mixture onto each chicken bundle and the tomatoes. Bake for 25 minutes, or until the chicken reaches an internal temperature of 165°F (75°C). Serve with any remaining balsamic, if desired.

Cooking Tip: *You can also add some halved baby potatoes to the baking sheet. Just toss with some of the balsamic mixture before adding! Spread them around the chicken with the tomatoes and roast with everything else.*

Sheet-Pan Pineapple Shrimp Fajitas

Egg Free, Low-Carb Option, Nut Free

Sheet-pan fajitas are something I make in our house almost weekly. I could literally eat Mexican food every day! This recipe makes it quite simple to have an amazing protein and veggie-packed meal on the table in 35 minutes. I added pineapple to give this sweet-and-spicy meal a fun twist. The flavor combination is absolutely incredible. You could serve these in burrito bowls, in Paleo tortillas, on top of a salad or simply straight off the pan!

Yield: *3-4 servings*
Hands-On Time: *10 minutes*
Hands-Off Time: *25 minutes*

2 tsp (5 g) chili powder

1 tsp cumin

1 tsp garlic powder

1 tsp onion powder

1 tsp sea salt

½ tsp oregano

½ tsp paprika

Dash of cayenne pepper (optional)

1 lb (454 g) fresh or frozen and thawed shrimp (pre-peeled, deveined and tails removed, see Cooking Tips)

2 tbsp (30 ml) olive oil or avocado oil, divided

2 bell peppers (any colors), sliced

1 red onion, sliced

1 (20-oz [567-g]) can pineapple tidbits in 100 percent pineapple juice, drained (see Cooking Tips)

Salad, burrito bowl or Paleo tortillas, for serving (optional)

Guacamole, for serving (optional)

Fresh cilantro, for serving (optional)

Preheat the oven to 400°F (200°C). Line a baking sheet with parchment paper or aluminum foil for easier cleanup, if desired.

In a small bowl, combine the chili powder, cumin, garlic powder, onion powder, salt, oregano, paprika and cayenne pepper (if using) and mix well.

Place the shrimp in a large bowl and coat with 1 tablespoon (15 ml) of the oil and half of the fajita seasoning. Mix well and place in the refrigerator.

In a large bowl, add the bell peppers, onion, pineapple tidbits and the remaining fajita seasoning and oil. Mix well and then dump out onto the baking sheet. Use a spatula to spread them out evenly. Bake for 15 minutes. Add the shrimp on top of the bell peppers, onion and pineapple. Cook for 10 minutes. If you want a bit of a char on everything, broil for 2 to 3 additional minutes. Serve on a salad, in a burrito bowl or on Paleo tortillas with guacamole, fresh cilantro or any other desired toppings.

Cooking Tips: *To use chicken instead of shrimp, cut 1 pound (454 g) of chicken breasts into strips and add them together with the onion, bell peppers and pineapple. Coat everything with all of the oil and all of the seasoning. Bake together for 25 minutes.*

For a low-carb option, omit the pineapple.

Ranch-Crusted Pork Tenderloin with Crispy Brussels Sprouts

Egg Free, Low Carb, Nut Free

Making roasted pork tenderloin used to intimidate me, until I realized how incredibly easy it is! These pork tenderloins are coated in a simple and delicious homemade ranch herb mixture and roasted alongside the Brussels sprouts. This one-pan meal is perfect for busy weeknights, yet fancy enough for a dinner party. Serve as is for a low-carb option, or add in some creamy "Cheesy" Mashed Potatoes (page 171)!

Yield: *3-4 servings*
Hands-On Time: *10 minutes*
Hands-Off Time: *30 minutes*

2 (1½-lb [680-g]) pork tenderloins

2 cloves garlic, minced

¾ tsp sea salt, divided

½ tsp dried minced onion

½ tsp dried parsley

½ tsp dried dill

½ tsp dried chives

½ tsp black pepper, divided

1 lb (454 g) Brussels sprouts, halved and ends removed (see Cooking Tip)

2 tbsp (30 ml) olive oil, divided

Preheat the oven to 425°F (220°C). Line a rimmed baking sheet with parchment paper for easy cleanup.

Trim the pork tenderloins and place them on the center of the baking sheet. In a small bowl, combine the garlic, ½ teaspoon of the salt, onion, parsley, dill, chives and ¼ teaspoon of the pepper. Spoon the mixture onto the pork tenderloins, and then use your hands to press it into the top and sides to make it stick.

In a large bowl, add the Brussels sprouts, 1 tablespoon (15 ml) of the olive oil and the remaining salt and pepper. Mix well. Place the Brussels sprouts all around the pork, cut side down (to ensure they get brown and crispy). Drizzle the remaining olive oil over the pork tenderloins. Bake for 30 minutes, or until the pork reaches an internal temperature of at least 145°F (63°C). Let the pork sit for 5 minutes before slicing and serving with the Brussels sprouts.

Cooking Tip: *This is also delicious with broccoli, but don't add it until there's only 15 minutes of cooking time left.*

Speedy
Skillets

Simple skillet meals are a weekly occurrence in our house. I love that they come together in one pan, which makes for easy cleanup. I made sure that all of the recipes in this chapter could be made in 30 minutes or less with 15 minutes or less of hands-on time, so that you would have plenty of options for busy weeknights!

My favorite types of skillets to use are a well-seasoned cast-iron pan and a nontoxic, nonstick pan for making things that stick easily, such as salmon.

Ground beef and ground pork are Paleo staples in our family. I've included a few quick prep recipes and ideas for using both, including Cottage Pie Bowls (page 38) and Korean Beef and Broccoli Bowls with Yum Yum Sauce (page 34). It can be helpful to keep ground meat in your freezer so you can pull it out and thaw it quickly when you don't have a dinner plan.

Shrimp also makes a great option when it comes to Paleo skillet cooking, since they don't take much time to fry up. I've included two delicious shrimp recipes in this chapter: The Ultimate Thai Basil Shrimp Curry (page 42) and Tuscan Shrimp with Sun-Dried Tomatoes and Spinach (page 46).

Some other favorites from this chapter include Chicken "Parm" and Cauliflower Gnocchi Skillet (page 41) and Creamy Salmon Piccata (page 37), which both taste decadent and delicious even without the dairy!

Korean Beef and Broccoli Bowls with Yum Yum Sauce

Egg-Free Option, Low Carb, Nut Free

This is such a flavorful dish that comes together in just 20 minutes. This is my go-to recipe when I have ground beef on hand. It has all of the flavors of beef and broccoli with a delicious creamy and tangy yum yum sauce. To save time, you can make the yum yum sauce up to 2 days ahead of time and store it in the refrigerator.

Yield: *3-4 servings*
Hands-On Time: *15 minutes*
Hands-Off Time: *5 minutes*

For the Beef and Broccoli
2 tsp (10 ml) sesame oil, divided

1 lb (454 g) ground beef

2 cloves garlic, minced

1 red bell pepper, diced

1 (12-oz [340-g]) package broccoli florets

For the Stir-Fry Sauce
⅓ cup (80 ml) coconut aminos

2 tsp (10 ml) sesame oil

½ tsp fish sauce

1 tsp rice vinegar

½ tsp crushed red pepper flakes

1 tsp ground ginger

1 tsp garlic powder

For the Yum Yum Sauce
½ cup (120 ml) mayonnaise (see Cooking Tip)

2 tbsp (30 ml) hot sauce

1 tbsp (15 ml) ketchup

1 tsp coconut aminos

½ tsp rice vinegar

For Serving
Cauliflower rice (optional)

To make the beef and broccoli, heat 1 teaspoon of the sesame oil in a large skillet over medium heat. Add the ground beef and sauté for 3 to 4 minutes, or until it is mostly browned and cooked through. Remove it from the skillet and set aside.

While the beef is browning, make the stir-fry sauce. In a medium bowl, whisk together the coconut aminos, sesame oil, fish sauce, rice vinegar, crushed red pepper flakes, ginger and garlic powder.

When the beef is browned and removed from the skillet, add the remaining sesame oil to the skillet with the garlic, bell pepper and broccoli florets. Stir for 1 to 2 minutes until the garlic is fragrant. Pour in half of the stir-fry sauce and stir. Cover the pan and cook over medium heat for 3 to 4 minutes, or until the broccoli becomes tender (but not mushy).

While the vegetables cook, make the yum yum sauce. In a small bowl, mix together the mayonnaise, hot sauce, ketchup, coconut aminos and rice vinegar.

Add the ground beef back into the skillet along with the remaining stir-fry sauce. Cook for 1 to 2 minutes until it's heated through. Serve the beef and broccoli mixture over cauliflower rice (optional) topped with the yum yum sauce.

Cooking Tip: *To make this meal egg free, use egg-free or vegan mayonnaise.*

Creamy Salmon Piccata

Egg Free, Low Carb, Nut-Free Option

In this simple skillet dish, salmon fillets are seared on both sides and then placed into a rich lemon cream sauce made from chicken broth and blended cashews. Capers and dill give this dish the perfect amount of flavor. It's delicious served over "Cheesy" Mashed Potatoes (page 171), with Spicy Roasted Broccolini (page 165) or over Garlic Cauliflower Mash (page 162).

Yield: *4 servings*
Hands-On Time: *10 minutes*
Hands-Off Time: *10 minutes*

1 tbsp (15 ml) olive oil or avocado oil

4 (6-oz [170-g]) salmon fillets

Salt and pepper, to taste

⅓ cup (49 g) raw, unsalted cashews (see Cooking Tips)

½ cup (120 ml) water

1 tbsp (15 ml) melted ghee

2 cloves garlic, minced

1 cup (240 ml) chicken broth

1½ tbsp (23 ml) lemon juice

1 tbsp (3 g) chopped fresh dill

2 tbsp (22 g) capers

2 tbsp (8 g) chopped parsley (optional)

Heat the oil in a large nonstick skillet over medium heat. Pat the salmon fillets dry with a paper towel. Sprinkle them with the salt and pepper. Cook the salmon skin side down for 3 to 4 minutes, and then flip and cook the other side for 3 minutes until cooked through. Remove the salmon to a plate and tent it with a piece of foil.

While the salmon is cooking, add the cashews and water to a high-speed blender. Blend on high for 1 minute, or until the cashews are completely smooth and creamy.

Remove any remaining oil from the skillet. Add the ghee and garlic. Cook over medium heat for 30 seconds. Add the chicken broth and lemon juice and scrape up any brown bits from the bottom of the pan. Pour the cashew cream into the pan and whisk it over medium heat for 1 to 2 minutes, or until thickened. Add the dill and capers, along with the salmon. Spoon some of the sauce over the salmon and serve topped with parsley, if desired.

Cooking Tips: *To make this nut free, omit the cashew cream. It will be more of a traditional piccata.*

If you do not have a high-speed blender like a Vitamix, I recommend soaking the cashews for at least 1 hour and then draining them before blending.

Cottage Pie Bowls

Egg Free, Low-Carb Option, Nut Free

Since traditional shepherd's pie is made with lamb, I decided to call this dish Cottage Pie Bowls since they are made with ground beef. In this deconstructed version, ground beef and veggies are cooked in a rich gravy and served over "Cheesy" Mashed Potatoes (page 171). No baking involved! You can also use ground lamb or ground turkey for this recipe.

Yield: *3-4 servings*
Hands-On Time: *15 minutes*
Hands-Off Time: *10 minutes*

1 tbsp (15 ml) olive oil

1 lb (454 g) ground beef

1 cup (160 g) diced onion

2 cloves garlic, minced

"Cheesy" Mashed Potatoes (page 171, optional, see Cooking Tip)

2 large carrots, peeled and diced

½ green bell pepper, diced

1 tsp dried thyme

1 tsp rosemary

1 tsp sea salt

1 tbsp (15 ml) coconut aminos

2 tbsp (32 g) tomato paste

1 cup (240 ml) beef or chicken broth

1 tsp arrowroot powder

1 tbsp (15 ml) water

Parsley, for serving (optional)

Heat the olive oil in a large skillet over medium heat. Add the ground beef, onion and garlic. Cook for 3 to 4 minutes, using a wooden spoon to break up the meat. If you're serving the meat mixture over the "Cheesy" Mashed Potatoes, bring your water to a boil and begin cooking the potatoes.

While the ground beef is browning, chop your carrots and green bell pepper. Add them to the skillet and stir. Add the thyme, rosemary, salt, coconut aminos and tomato paste. Stir everything well, and then pour the broth into the skillet.

Mix the arrowroot powder and water together in a small bowl to create a slurry. Bring the meat mixture to a boil and pour in the arrowroot slurry. Reduce the heat to medium-low and cover the skillet. Let it cook for 10 minutes, or until the carrots are tender. Serve over the mashed potatoes with parsley, if desired.

Cooking Tip: *To make this low carb, serve it over Garlic Cauliflower Mash (page 162) instead of the mashed potatoes.*

Chicken "Parm" and Cauliflower Gnocchi Skillet

Growing up, chicken parmesan was always my go-to meal to order when dining at an Italian restaurant. This better-for-you version uses a unique mixture of pork panko (crushed-up pork rinds) and Italian seasoning for the "breading" and a cashew cheese sauce instead of dairy. It gets baked in the oven alongside the cauliflower gnocchi, which makes for a quick and easy one-pan Italian meal!

Yield: *3-4 servings*
Hands-On Time: *15 minutes*
Hands-Off Time: *15 minutes*

For the Chicken

2 tbsp (30 ml) olive oil

1 egg, beaten

1 cup (56 g) homemade or store-bought pork panko (see Cooking Tips)

1 tsp Italian seasoning

½ tsp sea salt

½ tsp garlic powder

2 large chicken breasts, cut in half lengthwise to make 4 thinner breasts

2 cups (480 ml) marinara sauce (I like Rao's Homemade brand), divided

1 (12-oz [340-g]) package frozen cauliflower gnocchi (I like Trader Joe's brand)

For the "Cheese" Sauce

½ cup (73 g) raw, unsalted cashews

⅓ cup (80 ml) water

1 tbsp (5 g) nutritional yeast

½ tsp garlic powder

1 tbsp (15 ml) lemon juice

¼ tsp sea salt

Preheat the oven to 425°F (220°C).

To make the chicken, heat the olive oil over medium heat in a large cast-iron or oven-safe skillet. While the oil is heating, add the beaten egg to a shallow bowl. In a separate shallow bowl, add the pork panko, Italian seasoning, salt and garlic powder, and mix well. Dip each chicken breast half into the egg, and then into the panko mixture to coat completely. Add the chicken to the skillet, and cook for 2 to 3 minutes on each side. Remove to a plate and set aside.

While the chicken is cooking, make the "cheese" sauce. Add the cashews, water, nutritional yeast, garlic powder, lemon juice and salt to a high-speed blender. Blend until smooth.

Wipe any excess oil from the skillet using a paper towel. Add 1½ cups (360 ml) of the marinara sauce to the bottom of the skillet, and then add the frozen gnocchi on top. Nestle the chicken pieces in between the gnocchi. Spoon the remaining marinara sauce on top of each piece of chicken, followed by some of the "cheese" sauce. Bake the skillet for 15 minutes.

Cooking Tips: *Pork panko is available in many stores and online. If you prefer, you can make your own by crushing up pork rinds. Look for a brand where the ingredients are just pork and sea salt. (Epic brand Oven Baked Pork Rinds are great!)*

If you do not have a high-speed blender like a Vitamix, I recommend soaking the cashews for at least 1 hour and then draining them before blending.

The Ultimate Thai Basil Shrimp Curry

Egg Free, Low Carb, Nut Free

Thai food is one of my favorite things to cook AND eat! Most dishes use coconut milk, which is naturally gluten free and dairy free. This dish has so many fragrant spices with just a hint of heat. You can easily swap the veggies out for whatever you have on hand! It comes together in less than 20 minutes for an easy meal the entire family will love. Save even more time on a busy weeknight and prep the veggies the night before. Store them in an airtight container in the refrigerator until you're ready to start cooking.

Yield: *3-4 servings*
Hands-On Time: *10 minutes*
Hands-Off Time: *7 minutes*

2 tbsp (30 g) coconut oil, divided

1 lb (454 g) fresh or frozen and thawed shrimp (pre-peeled, deveined and tails removed)

2 cloves garlic, minced

1 red bell pepper, sliced

2 cups (182 g) broccoli florets

1 medium zucchini, cut into half-moon slices

½ tsp sea salt

1 tbsp (15 g) red Thai curry paste

1 tsp curry powder

1 (13.5-oz [398-ml]) can full-fat coconut milk (stir well before pouring)

1 tsp coconut aminos

¼ tsp fish sauce

¼ cup (10 g) chopped Thai basil

1 tbsp (15 ml) freshly squeezed lime juice

Cauliflower rice (optional)

Heat 1 tablespoon (15 ml) of the coconut oil in a skillet over medium-high heat. Add the shrimp and cook for 1 to 2 minutes on each side until they're cooked through and no longer translucent. Transfer to a plate using a slotted spoon and set aside.

Heat the remaining coconut oil. Add the garlic, red bell pepper, broccoli, zucchini, salt, Thai curry paste and curry powder. Stir for 2 to 3 minutes, or until the garlic and curry paste are fragrant. Add the coconut milk, coconut aminos and fish sauce. Stir, and then cover and bring to a boil. Once boiling, reduce the heat to medium-low and simmer for 5 to 7 minutes, or until the veggies are tender but not mushy. Add the cooked shrimp, the Thai basil (reserving a little for garnish) and the lime juice. Serve with a squeeze of lime and more fresh Thai basil. This is delicious on its own or over cauliflower rice!

Cooking Tip: *If you prefer to add some heat, add ½ teaspoon of cayenne pepper when you add the curry powder.*

Cashew Chicken and Green Bean Stir-Fry

Egg Free, Low-Carb Option

This quick Asian-inspired stir-fry comes together in less than 25 minutes and tastes just like Chinese takeout! The sauce is made from a combination of coconut aminos, sesame oil, rice vinegar and honey, which makes this completely gluten free and refined sugar free. Everything is cooked in one skillet for easy cleanup and minimal mess. I like to serve this over cauliflower rice.

Yield: *3-4 servings*
Hands-On Time: *15 minutes*
Hands-Off Time: *5 minutes*

1 lb (454 g) chicken breasts, cut into 1- to 2-inch (2.5- to 5-cm) chunks (see Cooking Tips)

½ tsp crushed red pepper flakes

2 tsp (5 g) tapioca starch

¼ cup (60 ml) coconut aminos, divided

2 tbsp (30 ml) sesame oil, divided

1 lb (454 g) green beans, halved

¼ tsp sea salt

1½ tbsp (23 ml) rice vinegar

2 cloves garlic, minced

1 tsp ground ginger

½ tsp fish sauce

1 tbsp (15 ml) honey (see Cooking Tips)

¾ cup (109 g) cashews

Add the cubed chicken to a large bowl and toss with the crushed red pepper flakes, tapioca starch and 1 tablespoon (15 ml) of the coconut aminos. Place the bowl in the refrigerator until you're ready to use it.

Heat 1 tablespoon (15 ml) of the sesame oil in a large nonstick skillet or wok over medium-high heat. Add the green beans and salt and cook for 3 to 4 minutes, stirring occasionally, until they are crisp-tender. While the green beans are cooking, in a small bowl, whisk the remaining coconut aminos, rice vinegar, garlic, ginger, fish sauce and honey.

Remove the green beans and set them aside. Add the remaining sesame oil to the skillet, followed by the chicken. Stir for 3 to 4 minutes, until the chicken is browned but not fully cooked through. Add the green beans, sauce and cashews to the skillet and stir. Cover and let everything cook for 5 minutes, or until the chicken reaches an internal temperature of 165°F (75°C).

Cooking Tips: *You can use 1 pound (454 g) of peeled and deveined shrimp in place of the chicken. Follow the same instructions, except only cook the shrimp for 1 to 2 minutes per side. After adding the green beans, sauce and cashews back into the pan, cover it and let everything cook for 5 minutes.*

Omit the honey to make this sugar free/low carb.

Tuscan Shrimp with Sun-Dried Tomatoes and Spinach

Egg Free, Low Carb, Nut Free

This quick skillet combines tender shrimp, sun-dried tomatoes and spinach in a delicious sauce with Italian spices and lemon. It cooks quickly so you can have dinner on the table in just 15 minutes! The lemon masks the flavor of the coconut milk, and the arrowroot slurry thickens it up nicely. This is one of those meals that definitely doesn't taste dairy free, but it is! I like to keep frozen shrimp in my freezer at all times, so I always have a quick last-minute meal option.

Yield: *3-4 servings*
Hands-On Time: *15 minutes*
Hands-Off Time: *none*

2 tbsp (24 g) ghee

1 lb (454 g) fresh or frozen and thawed shrimp (pre-peeled, deveined and tails removed)

4 cloves garlic, minced

⅓ cup (18 g) finely chopped sun-dried tomatoes

½ cup (120 ml) white wine

2 tbsp (30 ml) lemon juice

Zest from 1 lemon

1 (13.5-oz [398-ml]) can full-fat coconut milk (stir well before pouring)

½ tsp sea salt

1 tsp Italian seasoning

2 tightly packed cups (60 g) baby spinach

1 tsp arrowroot powder

1 tbsp (15 ml) water

Cauliflower rice or Garlic Cauliflower Mash (page 162), for serving

Heat the ghee in a large skillet over medium-high heat. Cook the shrimp for 1 to 2 minutes on each side, until they are no longer translucent. Remove the shrimp and set them aside on a plate.

Add the garlic and sun-dried tomatoes to the skillet and sauté for 1 to 2 minutes, until fragrant. Add the white wine and with a spoon scrape up any brown bits on the bottom of the skillet. Add the lemon juice, zest, coconut milk, salt and Italian seasoning. Add the shrimp back to the skillet along with the spinach and stir.

Mix the arrowroot powder and water together in a small bowl. Bring the skillet to a boil and add the arrowroot slurry. Stir while it thickens. This will happen quickly. Serve the shrimp over cauliflower rice or Garlic Cauliflower Mash (page 162).

Fast or Slow
Instant Pot and Slow Cooker Meals

There is something to be said for throwing some ingredients together in less than 15 minutes, pressing a button, walking away and coming back to a meal that tastes like you spent all day on it! That is the beauty of this chapter. I've included a combination of slow cooker and Instant Pot recipes with alternate instructions—including stovetop—where appropriate!

To save even more time, you can always chop your vegetables ahead of time and store them in the refrigerator or freezer until it's time to add everything to the slow cooker or Instant Pot.

There are lots of comforting soups and chilis packed with protein and veggies included in this chapter, such as Instant Pot Tuscan Sausage and Gnocchi Soup (page 61), Quick Chicken Pho (page 62), Creamy Tomato Soup (page 66) and Instant Pot Classic Beef Stew (page 54).

Beef and pork are often front and center in a lot of Paleo recipes. Cooking them in the slow cooker creates a melt-in-your-mouth texture with very minimal prep time and effort. Some favorites here include Better-For-You Mississippi Pot Roast (page 70), Slow Cooker Smothered Pork Chops (page 50), Easy Instant Pot Pulled BBQ Chicken (page 73) and Slow Cooker Barbacoa Tacos (page 65). These are true comfort foods that are completely dairy and gluten free.

Slow Cooker Smothered Pork Chops

Egg Free, Low Carb, Nut-Free Option

Growing up, my mom used to make this recipe with canned cream of mushroom soup, and it was one of my favorite meals! I knew I wanted to create my own version without any of the dairy, gluten or additives. The pork is slow-cooked all day and then we stir in a cashew "sour cream" sauce at the end. Make this meal even easier by making the cashew "sour cream" up to 24 hours in advance and store it in the refrigerator.

Yield: *3-4 servings*

Hands-On Time: *15 minutes*

Hands-Off Time: *8-10 hours on low (or 5-6 hours on high)*

For the Cashew "Sour Cream" (see Cooking Tips)

1 cup (150 g) raw, unsalted cashews

¾ cup (180 ml) water

½ tbsp (8 ml) lemon juice

For the Pork Chops

3-4 (1-inch [2.5-cm]-thick) boneless or bone-in pork chops

Sea salt, as needed

Black pepper, as needed

1 tbsp (15 ml) olive oil or melted ghee, plus more if needed

8 oz (226 g) white or cremini mushrooms, sliced

1 medium onion, diced

3 cloves garlic, minced

1½ cups (360 ml) chicken broth

1½ tsp (1 g) fresh thyme leaves or ¾ tsp dried thyme

Options for Serving

Garlic Cauliflower Mash (page 162)

"Cheesy" Mashed Potatoes (page 171)

Perfect Roasted Spaghetti Squash (page 169)

To make the cashew "sour cream," place the cashews into a bowl and cover with hot water. Let the cashews soak for the day while the pork chops cook.

To make the pork chops, season both sides of the pork chops with salt and pepper. Heat the olive oil or ghee in a large skillet over medium-high heat. Sear the pork chops for 2 minutes on each side.

While the pork chops are searing, chop the mushrooms and onion. Transfer the pork chops to the slow cooker. Add the onion, mushrooms and garlic to the same skillet. Add more oil if needed. Sauté for 3 to 4 minutes, then top the pork chops with the mixture. Add the chicken broth, thyme, salt and black pepper to the slow cooker. Cook on low for 8 to 10 hours or high for 5 to 6 hours.

When the pork chops are almost done cooking, finish the cashew "sour cream." Drain the cashews and add them to a high-speed blender along with the water and lemon juice. Blend on high for at least 1 minute, or until very smooth and creamy.

Remove the pork chops from the slow cooker and set them aside on a plate. Add the cashew "sour cream" to the slow cooker and whisk well until combined and the sauce is smooth. Place the pork chops back into the slow cooker. Serve over Garlic Cauliflower Mash (page 162), "Cheesy" Mashed Potatoes (page 171) or Perfect Roasted Spaghetti Squash (page 169) with extra sauce and mushrooms on top.

Cooking Tips: *To make this nut free, mix 1 cup (240 ml) of coconut cream with ½ tablespoon (8 ml) of lemon juice. Stir the mixture in at the end.*

To make this in the Instant Pot, soak the cashews for 1 hour while the pork chops cook. Follow the directions above for searing the pork chops and sautéing the onion, mushrooms and garlic. To keep the prep time down, do this in a separate skillet (otherwise you'd need to sear the pork in batches in the Instant Pot). Add the pork chops, onion, mushrooms, garlic, 2 cups (480 ml) of chicken broth, thyme, salt and black pepper to the Instant Pot. Stir well. Cook on manual high pressure for 60 minutes. Manually release the steam. Make the cashew "sour cream" per the directions above. Pour it into the pot and turn the Instant Pot to "saute". Cook for 5 minutes while stirring. The sauce will thicken upon standing.

Instant Pot Salsa Chicken Chili

Egg Free, Low Carb, Nut Free

Is there anything better than a big bowl of chili on a rainy day? This Mexican chili is dairy free and legume free, and it comes together quickly on the stovetop. It's got all of the flavors of chicken fajitas in soup form. Coconut milk and nutritional yeast give it the perfect amount of creaminess and "cheesy" flavor. I like to top mine with cilantro, extra coconut cream and avocado.

Yield: *6-8 servings*

Hands-On Time: *10 minutes*

Hands-Off Time: *35 minutes (including the time it takes for the Instant Pot to come to pressure)*

1 tbsp (15 ml) avocado oil

2 bell peppers (any color), diced

1 onion, diced

2 cloves garlic, minced

1½ lbs (680 g) boneless, skinless chicken breasts

1 (15.5-oz [439-g]) jar salsa

2 cups (480 ml) chicken broth

2 cloves garlic, minced

1 tsp cumin

2 tsp (5 g) chili powder

1 tsp onion powder

¼ tsp cayenne pepper

1 tsp oregano

½ tsp paprika

1 tsp sea salt

1 cup (240 ml) full-fat coconut milk (stir well before measuring)

2 tbsp (10 g) nutritional yeast

Juice from 1 lime

Avocado, for serving

Fresh cilantro, for serving

Set the Instant Pot to "sauté" mode. Add the avocado oil and let it heat up for 1 minute. Add the bell peppers, onion and garlic and sauté for 2 to 3 minutes. Place the chicken breasts on top of the bell peppers and onion. Pour the salsa over the chicken breasts. Pour in the chicken broth and add the garlic, cumin, chili powder, onion powder, cayenne pepper, oregano, paprika and salt, and give everything a stir. Lock the lid, turn the vent to "sealing," press "manual" (check that it's set to high pressure) and set the timer for 18 minutes.

Manually release the pressure, and then shred the chicken using two forks. You can either do this directly in the pot, or remove the chicken and shred it on a cutting board, and then add it back into the pot. Add the coconut milk, nutritional yeast and lime juice. Stir, and then serve topped with avocado and cilantro.

Cooking Tip: *To make this in a slow cooker, sauté the bell peppers, onion and garlic in a skillet on the stove, and then add them to the slow cooker. Add the chicken, salsa, chicken broth and spices. Cook on low for 7 to 8 hours or high for 3 to 4 hours. Shred the chicken, and then stir in the coconut milk, nutritional yeast and lime juice.*

Instant Pot Classic Beef Stew

Egg Free, Low-Carb Option, Nut Free

I've always been a meat-and-potatoes kinda girl, and this beef stew is one of my all-time favorite cozy meals! This stew is made in the Instant Pot in just 35 minutes (once it comes to pressure), but it tastes like it's been slow cooking all day. The meat is melt-in-your-mouth tender, and the gravy has an incredible savory flavor. The leftovers taste even better the next day! You can customize this by adding mushrooms or swapping the potatoes for sweet potatoes or butternut squash. Save time by omitting the sauté step in the beginning, and simply add everything to the pot and stir. This may result in slightly less flavor, but it will still be delicious! Save even more time by chopping your onions and carrots ahead of time and storing them in the refrigerator for up to 3 days before cooking.

Yield: *4-6 servings*

Hands-On Time: *15 minutes*

Hands-Off Time: *55 minutes (including the time it takes for the Instant Pot to come to pressure)*

1½ lbs (680 g) stew meat, cut into even-sized cubes

2 tbsp (16 g) arrowroot powder, divided

Sea salt, as needed, plus 1 tsp, divided

Black pepper, as needed

1 tbsp (15 ml) melted ghee or olive oil

1 medium yellow onion, chopped

3 cloves garlic, minced

5 carrots, peeled and cut into 1-inch (2.5-cm) pieces

3 cups (450 g) quartered mini gold potatoes (see Cooking Tips)

2 tbsp (32 g) tomato paste

1½ cups (360 ml) beef or chicken broth

1 tbsp (15 ml) hot sauce

1 tbsp (15 ml) coconut aminos

2 tsp (1 g) fresh thyme leaves

1 bay leaf

2 tbsp (30 ml) water

Fresh parsley, for serving

In a large bowl, toss the stew meat with 1 tablespoon (8 g) of the arrowroot powder. Sprinkle with a bit of salt and pepper. Set the Instant Pot to "sauté" mode. Add the ghee or olive oil and allow it to heat up. Add the onion, garlic and stew meat. Stir occasionally for 2 to 3 minutes. Meanwhile, chop your carrots and potatoes.

Add the tomato paste and stir until combined. Press "keep warm/cancel," and add the carrots, potatoes, broth, hot sauce, aminos, thyme, 1 teaspoon of salt and the bay leaf. Give it a quick stir, and then lock the lid and turn the vent to "sealing." Press "meat/stew" (check that it's on high pressure) and set the timer for 35 minutes. Once it's done cooking, let the Instant Pot gradually release for 10 minutes, and then manually release the pressure. Press "sauté" and let the stew come to a boil. In a small bowl, mix the remaining arrowroot powder with the water to create a slurry. Add the slurry to the pot and stir for 1 to 2 minutes until the stew thickens. Remove the bay leaf and serve the stew with fresh parsley.

Cooking Tips: *To make this in a slow cooker, toss the stew meat with 1 tablespoon (8 g) of the arrowroot powder and sprinkle with salt and pepper. Heat a large skillet over medium heat and add 1 tablespoon (15 ml) of cooking fat of choice. Add the onion, garlic and stew meat. Let it cook for 4 to 5 minutes, stirring occasionally, until browned. Meanwhile, chop your carrots and potatoes. Add the onion, garlic and beef to the slow cooker along with the carrots, potatoes, tomato paste, broth, hot sauce, aminos, thyme, 1 teaspoon of sea salt and the bay leaf. Stir and cook on low for 8 to 10 hours or high for 4 to 5 hours. When finished, turn the slow cooker to high heat. Add the arrowroot slurry mixture and stir occasionally for 10 minutes, or until the stew is thickened.*

To make this low carb, omit the potatoes.

Instant Pot Butternut Squash Curry

Egg Free, Nut-Free Option, Vegan

I'm a huge fan of any curry dish, or really any dish that involves cauliflower rice with a decadent sauce! This butternut squash curry is a delicious plant-based comfort food meal that comes together quickly. It's sweet, spicy and packed with flavor. The pomegranates and cashews give it a nice crunch! I like to serve it over cauliflower rice. To save time, use pre-cubed butternut squash, which can be found in the refrigerated produce section of most grocery stores.

Yield: *3-4 servings*

Hands-On Time: *10 minutes*

Hands-Off Time: *15 minutes*
(including the time it takes for the Instant Pot to come to pressure)

1 tbsp (15 g) coconut oil

½ onion, diced

3 cloves garlic, minced

2 tsp (4 g) grated ginger

2 tbsp (30 g) red Thai curry paste

4 cups (560 g) cubed butternut squash

¼ cup (60 ml) tomato sauce

1 (13.5-oz [398-ml]) can full-fat coconut milk (stir well before pouring)

½ cup (120 ml) water

2 tsp (4 g) curry powder

½ tsp sea salt

1 tsp coriander

1 tbsp (15 ml) maple syrup (see Cooking Tips)

2 cups (60 g) raw spinach

Cauliflower rice, for serving

Chopped cashews, for serving (see Cooking Tips)

Cilantro, for serving

Pomegranate arils, for serving

Set the Instant Pot to "sauté" mode. Heat the coconut oil in the Instant Pot. Add the onion and stir for 1 to 2 minutes. Add the garlic and ginger and stir for 30 seconds, or until fragrant. Add the red curry paste and stir, scraping up any brown bits from the bottom of the pot. Add the squash, tomato sauce, coconut milk, water, curry powder, salt, coriander and maple syrup. Stir well to combine.

Lock the lid, turn the vent to "sealing," press "manual" (check that it's set to high pressure) and set the timer for 4 minutes. Manually release the pressure. Press "keep warm/cancel," add the spinach and stir. Serve over cauliflower rice with chopped cashews, cilantro and pomegranate arils.

Cooking Tips: *To make this on the stove, in a large pot, heat the coconut oil over medium heat. Add the onion and stir for 2 to 3 minutes. Add the garlic and ginger and stir for 30 seconds, or until fragrant. Add the curry paste and stir. Add the remaining ingredients (minus the spinach), stir and cook over medium heat for 15 minutes, or until the squash is tender but not too soft. Add the spinach and stir.*

Omit the maple syrup for a sugar-free recipe.

Omit the cashews to make this nut free.

Slow Cooker Classic Italian Meatballs

Low Carb, Nut-Free Option

Growing up, my all-time favorite meal to order at any restaurant was spaghetti and meatballs! This is my go-to Italian meatball recipe, which has all of the flavors without any of the breadcrumbs, gluten, dairy or grains. The best part about this recipe is that it's so incredibly easy! You place the uncooked meatballs directly into the slow cooker along with a homemade marinara sauce, and let it work its magic. The combination of ground beef and ground pork gives both the meatballs and the sauce incredible flavor. Save time by using two 28-ounce (790-g) jars of marinara sauce instead of making your own. This dish is delicious served over Perfect Roasted Spaghetti Squash (page 169). Mangia!

Yield: *20-24 meatballs (depending on how large you make them)*
Hands-On Time: *15 minutes*
Hands-Off Time: *3-4 hours*

For the Meatballs

Avocado or olive oil cooking spray

1 lb (454 g) ground beef

1 lb (454 g) ground pork

2 eggs

½ cup (48 g) almond flour (see Cooking Tips)

2 tbsp (30 ml) coconut aminos

¼ cup (40 g) minced onion

¼ cup (13 g) loosely packed chopped fresh parsley

1½ tsp (9 g) sea salt

2 tsp (5 g) garlic powder

2 tsp (4 g) Italian seasoning

For the Sauce

3 cups (720 ml) marinara sauce (I like Rao's Homemade brand)

1 (28-oz [794-g]) can chopped tomatoes

2 cloves garlic, minced

½ tsp sea salt

¼ cup (20 g) nutritional yeast

1 tsp Italian seasoning

To make the meatballs, spray the inside of your slow cooker with the avocado or olive oil cooking spray. In a large bowl, combine the ground beef and pork, eggs, almond flour, aminos, onion, parsley, salt, garlic powder and Italian seasoning. Mix well using your hands. Form the mixture into balls (about 2 inches [5 cm] wide) and place them directly into the slow cooker by covering the bottom first then stacking them as necessary.

To make the sauce, in a large bowl, mix together the sauce, tomatoes, garlic, salt, nutritional yeast and Italian seasoning. Pour the sauce over the meatballs and place the cover on the slow cooker. Cook on high for 3 to 4 hours. (Do not stir until it's done!)

Cooking Tips: *You can freeze the meatballs and sauce for up to 3 months.*

To make this nut free, use 2½ tablespoons (18 g) of coconut flour in place of the almond flour.

Instant Pot Tuscan Sausage and Gnocchi Soup

Egg Free, Nut Free

This hearty soup combines Italian sausage, spinach and cauliflower gnocchi in a delicious creamy broth—very similar to zuppa Toscana. Paleo cauliflower gnocchi can be found in the freezer section at some grocery stores, such as Trader Joe's, or online. This soup can be made in less than 30 minutes, and it has the most incredible Italian flavors. It can be stored in the refrigerator for up to 3 days. Please note that the gnocchi does soften the longer it sits in the broth, but it's still delicious!

Yield: *3-4 servings*

Hands-On Time: *10 minutes*

Hands-Off Time: *25 minutes (including the time it takes for the Instant Pot to come to pressure)*

1 tbsp (15 ml) olive oil

1 lb (454 g) Italian sausage, casings removed (see Cooking Tip)

1 small onion, diced

3 cloves garlic, minced

3 cups (720 ml) chicken broth

1 (14.5-oz [411-g]) can diced tomatoes with juices

2 tsp (4 g) Italian seasoning

½ tsp sea salt

1 (12-oz [340-g]) package frozen cauliflower gnocchi (I like Trader Joe's brand)

3 tightly packed cups (90 g) raw baby spinach or kale

1 cup (240 ml) full-fat coconut milk (stir well before measuring)

Set the Instant Pot to "sauté" mode. Heat the olive oil in the Instant Pot. Add the sausage, onion and garlic. Cook for 4 to 5 minutes, breaking the sausage up with a wooden spoon. Press "keep warm/cancel" and add the chicken broth, diced tomatoes, Italian seasoning and salt. Lock the lid, and turn the vent to "sealing." Press "manual" (check that it's set to high pressure) and set the timer for 10 minutes.

Manually release the pressure, and then press the "sauté" button. Add the frozen cauliflower gnocchi, spinach and coconut milk. The gnocchi will cook very quickly—within 2 to 3 minutes.

Cooking Tip: *Try to look for Italian sausage without sugar, if possible, to keep it Paleo.*

Quick Chicken Pho

Egg-Free Option, Low Carb, Nut Free

Pho is the ultimate comfort food on a rainy day or if you aren't feeling 100 percent. If you aren't familiar with it, pho is a Vietnamese soup consisting of broth, rice noodles, herbs and meat. Typically the broth is simmered for hours, which gives it incredible flavor. In this Instant Pot grain-free version, the herbs and spices are quickly sautéed and then pressure-cooked with the chicken and broth. This results in a quick, flavorful soup that is ready in less than 30 minutes!

Yield: *3-4 servings*

Hands-On Time: *10 minutes*

Hands-Off Time: *17 minutes*
(including the time it takes the Instant Pot to come to pressure)

1 tbsp (15 ml) olive oil

3 cloves garlic, minced

½ medium onion, diced

2 whole star anise or ½ tsp Chinese five spice powder

2 whole cloves or ½ tsp Chinese five spice powder or a pinch of ground cloves

1 lb (454 g) boneless, skinless chicken breasts (or thighs) cut into 3-inch (8-cm) pieces (see Cooking Tips)

1 tbsp (6 g) grated ginger

1 tbsp (15 ml) fish sauce

2 tbsp (30 ml) coconut aminos

4 cups (960 ml) chicken broth

2 large eggs (optional, see Cooking Tips)

2 cups (340 g) pre-spiralized zucchini noodles

½ cup (8 g) cilantro leaves, for serving

Jalapeño slices, for serving (optional)

Sliced limes, for serving (optional)

Sliced radishes, for serving (optional)

Set the Instant Pot to "sauté" mode. Add the olive oil, garlic, onion, star anise and cloves. Sauté for 2 to 3 minutes, until fragrant. Add the chicken, ginger, fish sauce, aminos and chicken broth. Press "keep warm/cancel," lock the lid and turn the vent to "sealing." Press "manual" (check that it's set to high pressure), and set the timer for 12 minutes. When done, manually release the pressure, and then shred the chicken with two forks.

While the soup is cooking, make the eggs (if using). Bring a small pot of water to a boil. Use a spoon to gently place the eggs into the pot. Cook for 6 minutes, and then transfer to an ice bath. (Cooking the eggs for 6 minutes gives them a soft-cooked consistency. Add an extra minute if you prefer the yolks to be completely done.) Peel the eggs, and cut them in half.

To serve the soup, divide the raw zucchini noodles into bowls. Spoon some of the shredded chicken into the bowls and then pour the broth over top. It will start to cook the zucchini noodles right in the bowl. Top with the eggs (if using), cilantro, sliced jalapeño, limes and/or radishes.

Cooking Tips: *To make this on the stove, in a large pot, sauté the garlic, onion, star anise and cloves over medium heat. Add the remaining ingredients (minus the zucchini noodles and garnishes). Bring to a boil, and then cook over medium heat for 20 minutes. Shred the chicken, and follow the remaining steps listed above.*

To make this with thinly sliced beef or thawed shrimp instead of chicken, simply add them to the pot after the broth is done cooking. Let them cook on the sauté function (or over medium heat) for 1 to 2 minutes, or until cooked through.

Omit the eggs to make this recipe egg free.

Slow Cooker Barbacoa Tacos

Egg Free, Low Carb, Nut Free

Many versions of this slow-cooked shredded beef are made with canned chipotle peppers in adobo sauce, which often contain additives like corn syrup and sugar. Here we use a combination of chipotle powder, tomato paste and coconut aminos to replace this! This step is optional, but I love to add the shredded beef to a pan and broil it for 10 minutes to get it nice and crispy. Here I used grain-free flour tortillas, but you can also serve this over cauliflower rice or in lettuce wraps!

Yield: *6-8 servings*
Hands-On Time: *10 minutes*
Hands-Off Time: *8-10 hours*

3 lbs (1.4 kg) chuck roast or any large cut of beef such as round roast, etc.

3 cloves garlic, minced

1 onion, diced

2 bay leaves

¾ cup (180 ml) beef broth

2 tsp (4 g) chipotle powder

1 tbsp (6 g) cumin

2 tbsp (32 g) tomato paste

2 tsp (12 g) sea salt

2 tsp (4 g) oregano

½ tsp allspice

1 tbsp (15 ml) apple cider vinegar

2 tbsp (30 ml) lime juice

1 tbsp (15 ml) coconut aminos

For Serving
Grain-free tortillas (I like Siete Foods brand)

Diced red onion (optional)

Avocado (optional)

Fresh cilantro (optional)

Lime wedges (optional)

Add the beef, garlic, onion and bay leaves to the slow cooker. In a medium bowl, mix together the beef broth, chipotle powder, cumin, tomato paste, salt, oregano, allspice, apple cider vinegar, lime juice and coconut aminos. Pour over the beef. Cook on low for 8 to 10 hours or high for 4 to 5 hours.

Shred the beef using two forks and discard the bay leaves. Optional: Transfer the shredded beef to a foil-lined baking sheet and broil for 10 minutes until crispy. Serve in the tortillas with diced red onion, avocado, cilantro and/or lime wedges. This barbacoa can be stored in the refrigerator for up to 5 days.

Cooking Tip: *To make this in an Instant Pot, cut the beef into 5 to 6 pieces. Add the garlic, onion and beef chunks to the Instant Pot. Mix the sauce, and pour it over everything. Give it a good stir so the sauce is coating the bottom of the pan. Press "manual" (check that it's set to high pressure) and set the timer for 1 hour. Manually release the pressure. Follow the remaining instructions.*

Creamy Tomato Soup

Egg Free, Low Carb, Nut Free, Vegan Option

There are few things more comforting than a big bowl of homemade tomato soup! This version combines whole, peeled tomatoes with Italian spices, chicken broth and coconut milk. Everything is cooked in the Instant Pot and then blended using a handheld immersion blender. There's no need to transfer it to your blender and make a mess! Topped with fresh basil and cracked black pepper, this makes a perfect appetizer or main dish any time of year!

Yield: *4-6 servings*

Hands-On Time: *10 minutes*

Hands-Off Time: *18 minutes*
(including the time it takes the Instant Pot to come to pressure)

1 tbsp (15 ml) olive oil

½ large onion, diced

2 cloves garlic, minced

2 tbsp (32 g) tomato paste

1 (28-oz [794-g]) can whole, peeled San Marzano tomatoes

2 cups (480 ml) chicken broth (see Cooking Tips)

½ tbsp (3 g) Italian seasoning

1 tbsp (13 g) coconut sugar (substitute 1 tbsp [15 ml] coconut aminos to make this sugar free)

1 tsp sea salt

½ tsp crushed red pepper flakes

½ tsp paprika

1 (13.5-oz [398-ml]) can full-fat coconut milk (stir well before pouring)

¼ cup (10 g) chopped fresh basil, for serving

Cracked black pepper, to taste

Set the Instant Pot to "sauté" mode and heat the olive oil. Add the onion and garlic and sauté for 3 to 4 minutes, or until fragrant. Stir in the tomato paste, and then add the canned tomatoes with their juices, chicken broth, Italian seasoning, coconut sugar, salt, crushed red pepper flakes and paprika. Press "keep warm/cancel," and then lock the lid and turn the vent to "sealing." Press "manual" (check that it's set to high pressure), and set the timer for 12 minutes.

Manually release the steam, and then add the can of coconut milk. Use an immersion blender to carefully blend the soup until it's completely smooth. Serve with fresh basil and cracked black pepper.

Cooking Tips: *To make this on the stove, heat the olive oil in a large pot over medium heat. Add the onion and garlic and stir for 3 to 4 minutes. Stir in the tomato paste, and then add the canned tomatoes, chicken broth, Italian seasoning, coconut sugar, salt, crushed red pepper flakes and paprika. Stir well and bring everything to a boil. Reduce the heat to medium-low and cover. Cook for 30 minutes. Add the coconut milk, and use an immersion blender to blend the soup until it's completely smooth.*

To make this vegan, use vegetable broth instead of chicken broth.

Instant Pot Orange-Sesame Chicken

Egg Free, Nut Free

Chinese food is one of those things I could eat every single day of my life. Unfortunately, most of it isn't gluten free. I love getting creative and finding ways to recreate classic Asian-inspired dishes with healthier ingredients. This orange chicken is tangy, sweet and sour . . . and it also makes amazing leftovers. It couldn't be any simpler to throw together, making it a perfect option for busy weeknights. I like to serve it with cauliflower rice, but it would also be delicious over some Perfect Roasted Spaghetti Squash (page 169). Chopsticks are fun, but optional!

Yield: *3-4 servings*

Hands-On Time: *15 minutes*

Hands-Off Time: *20 minutes (including the time for the Instant Pot to come to pressure)*

2 tbsp (30 ml) sesame oil, divided

2 lbs (907 g) chicken breasts, cut into 1-inch (2.5-cm) cubes

½ cup (120 ml) orange juice

3 cloves garlic, minced

¼ cup (60 ml) coconut aminos

1 tsp rice vinegar

1 tbsp (6 g) grated ginger

¼ cup (60 ml) tomato sauce

2 tbsp (30 ml) honey (see Cooking Tips)

¼ tsp crushed red pepper flakes

½ tsp sea salt

1 tsp orange zest

1 tbsp (8 g) arrowroot powder

2 tbsp (30 ml) water

Sesame seeds, for serving (optional)

Chopped green onions, for serving (optional)

Cauliflower rice or Perfect Roasted Spaghetti Squash (page 169), for serving (optional)

Set the Instant Pot to "sauté" mode. Add 1 tablespoon (15 ml) of the sesame oil to the pot. Add the chicken and sauté for 3 to 4 minutes, or until the chicken is just beginning to brown. Press "keep warm/cancel."

In a large bowl, mix together the orange juice, garlic, aminos, remaining sesame oil, rice vinegar, ginger, tomato sauce, honey, crushed red pepper flakes, salt and orange zest. Pour the mixture over the chicken and use a spoon to scrape up any brown bits from the bottom of the pot. Stir everything well, and then lock the lid and turn the vent to "sealing." Press "manual" (check that it's set to high pressure), and set the timer for 6 minutes.

Quick release the steam. Remove the chicken using a slotted spoon and set aside on a plate. Press the "sauté" button and bring the sauce to a boil. In a small bowl, stir the arrowroot powder and the water together. Pour it into the Instant Pot. Stir for 2 to 3 minutes, until the sauce thickens. It will also thicken more upon standing. Add the chicken back into the pot and stir. Press "keep warm/cancel." Serve the chicken topped with sesame seeds and green onions over cauliflower rice or spaghetti squash noodles (if desired).

Cooking Tips: *To make this on the stove, heat 1 tablespoon (15 ml) of the sesame oil in a large skillet over medium heat. Mix up the sauce ingredients. Add the chicken to the skillet and cook for 3 to 4 minutes, until it starts to brown. Add the sauce and stir, scraping up any brown bits from the bottom of the pan. Cook over medium heat for 12 minutes, or until the chicken is cooked through. Remove the chicken using a slotted spoon. Combine the arrowroot powder and water to create a slurry, and add it to the pot. Stir for 2 to 3 minutes until the sauce is thickened. Add the chicken back in and stir.*

Omit the honey for a sugar-free version.

Better-For-You Mississippi Pot Roast

Egg Free, Low Carb, Nut Free

I used to make a not-so-healthy version of Mississippi pot roast using butter, a packet of au jus mix and a packet of ranch dressing mix. Unfortunately, those mixes are filled with gluten and ingredients that don't make me feel great! I knew I had to create a version that still had all of the flavors without any of the junk. This beef dish requires very minimal prep time and is one of my favorite "set it and forget it" meals! It is truly the ultimate comfort food. I like to serve it over Garlic Cauliflower Mash (page 162) or "Cheesy" Mashed Potatoes (page 171).

Yield: *4-6 servings*
Hands-On Time: *10 minutes*
Hands-Off Time: *8-10 hours on low (or 4-5 hours on high)*

For the Pot Roast

3 lb (1.4 kg) chuck roast

½ cup (120 ml) sugar-free beef broth

1 tbsp (15 ml) coconut aminos

1 tsp dried parsley

1 tsp dried chives

1 tsp dried dill weed

2 tsp (3 g) garlic powder

1 tsp onion powder

1 tsp dried onion flakes

1½ tsp (9 g) sea salt

½ tsp black pepper

3 tbsp (45 ml) melted ghee

8 pepperoncinis

For the Gravy

1 cup (240 ml) juices from the slow cooker once the beef is done cooking

1 tbsp (8 g) arrowroot powder

2 tbsp (30 ml) water

To make the pot roast, add the chuck roast to the slow cooker. Pour the beef broth and coconut aminos over the top. Sprinkle the parsley, chives, dill, garlic powder, onion powder, onion flakes, salt and pepper on top of the beef. Add the ghee on top of the beef, and place the pepperoncinis around the beef. Cook on low for 8 to 10 hours or high for 4 to 5 hours. Remove the roast and transfer it to a cutting board. Shred it using two forks.

To make the gravy, transfer 1 cup (240 ml) of the juices from the slow cooker to a small saucepan. In a small bowl, combine the arrowroot powder and water to make a slurry. Bring the juices to a boil, and then stir in the slurry. Reduce the heat to medium-low, and stir it until your desired consistency has been reached.

Serve the shredded beef on top of your desired side dish with gravy and pepperoncinis from the pot.

Cooking Tip: *To make this in an Instant Pot, cut the beef into 4 even pieces. Add 1 cup (240 ml) of beef broth, and keep all other measurements the same. Lock the lid, turn the vent to "sealing," press "manual" (check that it's set to high pressure) and set the timer for 60 minutes. Then let it slow release for 15 minutes. Follow the rest of the directions to shred the beef and make the gravy.*

Easy Instant Pot Pulled BBQ Chicken

Low Carb, Egg Free, Nut Free

A simple Instant Pot recipe that involves zero sautéing time is my love language! This BBQ chicken could not be easier to throw together, and it's a perfect versatile dish for busy weeknights. I love serving it with Sweet and Spicy Oven-Baked Sweet Potato Fries (page 158) and Simple Classic Coleslaw (page 165), but it would also be delicious in lettuce wraps, with cauliflower rice, over "Cheesy" Mashed Potatoes (page 171) or stuffed into sweet potatoes.

Yield: *4–6 servings*

Hands-On Time: *5 minutes*

Hands-Off Time: *35 minutes (including the time it takes for the Instant Pot to come to pressure)*

½ cup (120 ml) chicken broth

1½ lbs (680 g) boneless, skinless chicken breasts, cut into 2-inch (5-cm) pieces

½ red onion, diced

1 cup (240 ml) sugar-free BBQ sauce (I like Tessemae's)

2 tbsp (30 ml) maple syrup or 2 tbsp (30 g) coconut sugar (see Cooking Tips)

2 tsp (10 ml) coconut aminos

½ tsp garlic powder

½ tsp paprika

¼ tsp sea salt

Add the chicken broth, chicken breast pieces, red onion, BBQ sauce, maple syrup, aminos, garlic powder, paprika and salt to the Instant Pot. Do not stir. This is important to ensure the Instant Pot is able to come to pressure.

Lock the lid and turn the vent to "sealing." Press "manual" (check that it's set to high pressure), and set the timer for 15 minutes. Let it slow release for 10 minutes, and then manually release the rest of the pressure. Remove the chicken breast pieces with a slotted spoon to a cutting board, and use two forks to shred them. Return the shredded chicken to the pot and stir into the sauce. Serve with desired side dishes.

Cooking Tips: *To make this in a slow cooker, add all of the ingredients as listed above to the slow cooker. You do not need to cut the chicken breasts into pieces; they can be full size. Cook on low for 8 to 10 hours or high for 4 to 5 hours. Remove the chicken breasts to a cutting board and use two forks to shred them. Return the shredded chicken to the pot and stir into the sauce.*

Omit the maple syrup or coconut sugar for a sugar-free recipe.

Instant Pot Lemon Chicken and "Rice" Soup

Egg Free, Low Carb, Nut Free

They say chicken soup is good for the soul, and they are right! Nothing beats a comforting bowl of soup when you are feeling under the weather or when it's chilly outside. I love the addition of the tart lemon and fresh dill in this soup. Instead of regular rice, I use cauliflower rice to keep it low carb and grain free. To save time, you can use 1½ cups (203 g) of pre-chopped mirepoix (diced celery, carrots and onion mix) instead of the un-prepped veggies.

Yield: *6-8 servings*

Hands-On Time: *10 minutes*

Hands-Off Time: *32 minutes (including the time it takes the Instant Pot to come to pressure)*

1 tbsp (15 ml) olive oil or melted ghee

2 stalks celery, diced

2 large carrots, peeled and diced

½ medium onion, diced

2 cloves garlic, minced

1½ lbs (680 g) chicken breasts or boneless, skinless chicken thighs

5 cups (1.2 L) chicken broth

1 tsp thyme

2 tsp (12 g) sea salt, plus more to taste

12 oz (340 g) frozen cauliflower rice (see Cooking Tips)

1 tbsp (3 g) fresh dill

2 tbsp (30 ml) freshly squeezed lemon juice

Lemon slices, for serving

Fresh parsley, for serving

Set the Instant Pot to "sauté" mode, and add the olive oil or ghee. Once heated, add the celery, carrots and onion. Sauté for 2 to 3 minutes, or until they begin to soften. Add the garlic and continue to stir for 30 seconds, or until it becomes fragrant. Add the chicken, making sure to lay the pieces side by side without overlapping. Add the chicken broth, thyme and salt. Lock the lid, turn the vent to "sealing," press "manual" (check that it's set to high pressure) and set the timer for 12 minutes.

Let the Instant Pot gradually release for 10 minutes, and then manually release the rest of the pressure. Transfer the chicken to a cutting board and shred it using two forks. Return the shredded chicken to the pot. Set the Instant Pot to "sauté" mode, and add the frozen cauliflower rice, fresh dill and lemon juice. Cook for 3 to 4 minutes, stirring occasionally, until the cauliflower rice is cooked and heated through. Serve with slices of lemon and fresh parsley.

Cooking Tips: *To make this on the stove, follow the sauté directions above using a large stock pot. Add the chicken, chicken broth, thyme and salt. Bring to a boil, and then reduce the heat to medium and cover. Cook for 30 minutes. Remove the chicken and shred it using two forks. Return the chicken to the pot along with the cauliflower rice, dill and lemon juice. Cook for an additional 3 to 4 minutes, or until the cauliflower rice is cooked through.*

You can replace the cauliflower rice with zucchini noodles (or any veggie noodle of choice) if preferred! Simply place them in the pot during the last 3 to 4 minutes of cooking time and cook until tender.

One-Pot *Wonders*

In this chapter, you'll find lots of hearty recipes that can all be made in one pot with very little hands-on time. A 5- or 6-quart (5- or 6-L) Dutch oven works great for most of these recipes, but if you do not have one, you can certainly use any regular pot (making sure it's oven safe where necessary). I've included Instant Pot directions where appropriate, but many of these recipes work best when made on the regular old stovetop or in the oven.

This chapter includes a variety of comforting homestyle meals that are grain free, dairy free and gluten free without sacrificing taste! I've also included tips for saving time with these recipes, like chopping your vegetables ahead of time and storing them in the refrigerator until you're ready to start cooking, and using pre-spiralized or pre-chopped vegetables from the grocery store.

Some favorites from this chapter include Loaded Potato and Broccoli "Cheese" Soup (page 81), Zoodles with Italian Sausage, Fennel and Mushrooms (page 82) and Perfect Dutch Oven Roasted Chicken (page 89).

Quick Cuban Picadillo

Egg Free, Low-Carb Option, Nut Free

Picadillo is a tomato-based ground beef dish traditionally served in many Latin American countries. It has incredible flavor from the raisins, olives and spices. I use a combination of ground pork and ground beef, but you can certainly use just one type. This dish is so versatile and can be served in so many different ways. Here I served it with cauliflower rice and plantain chips (store bought or homemade) for dipping! This recipe comes together quickly and is perfect for busy weeknights!

Yield: *4-6 servings*
Hands-On Time: *10 minutes*
Hands-Off Time: *25 minutes*

2 tbsp (30 ml) olive oil

1 lb (454 g) ground beef

1 lb (454 g) ground pork

1 medium onion, diced

4 cloves garlic, minced

1 red bell pepper, diced

⅓ cup (48 g) raisins (see Cooking Tips)

½ cup (90 g) sliced pitted green olives

2 tbsp (15 ml) coconut aminos

1 (15-oz [444-ml]) can tomato sauce

½ cup (120 ml) beef broth

2 tsp (2 g) cumin

1 tsp oregano

1 bay leaf

1½ tsp (9 g) sea salt

½ tsp cinnamon

¼ tsp cayenne pepper

Cauliflower rice, for serving (optional)

Plantain chips, for serving (optional)

Heat the olive oil in a large Dutch oven or deep skillet over medium-high heat. Add the ground beef, ground pork, onion and garlic. Sauté for 5 to 7 minutes, using a wooden spoon to break up the meat. Once it is mostly browned, add the bell pepper, raisins, olives, coconut aminos, tomato sauce, beef broth, cumin, oregano, bay leaf, salt, cinnamon and cayenne pepper. Stir well. Bring everything to a boil, and then cover and reduce the heat to medium-low. Simmer for 15 to 20 minutes. Remove the bay leaf. Serve with cauliflower rice and plantain chips, if desired.

Cooking Tips: *To make this in an Instant Pot, set the pot to "sauté" mode. Cook the oil, ground pork, ground beef, onion and garlic for 5 to 7 minutes. Add 1 cup (240 ml) of beef broth plus the remaining ingredients and stir. Lock the lid, turn the vent to "sealing," press "manual" (check that it's set to high pressure) and set the timer for 15 minutes. Manually release the steam, stir and serve.*

To keep this low carb, omit the raisins.

Loaded Potato and Broccoli "Cheese" Soup

Egg Free, Nut-Free Option, Vegan Option

Growing up, two of my favorite hearty soups were loaded baked potato soup and cheesy broccoli cheddar soup. Unfortunately, the flour and dairy don't work for me anymore, so I decided to create a combination of both soups without either ingredient! A mixture of pureed potatoes, cashews and nutritional yeast create the most perfect creamy, "cheesy" flavored soup. Crispy bacon is the perfect garnish for many things in life, but especially this dish! To save time, you can make the bacon ahead of time.

Yield: *4-6 servings*

Hands-On Time: *15 minutes*

Hands-Off Time: *30 minutes*

8 pieces sugar-free bacon (see Cooking Tips)

½ medium onion, diced

3 carrots, peeled and diced

2 lbs (907 g) russet potatoes (3 medium or 4 small), peeled and cut into 1-inch (2.5-cm) cubes

1 tbsp (15 ml) melted ghee or olive oil

2 cloves garlic, minced

4 cups (960 ml) chicken broth (see Cooking Tips)

1 tsp paprika

1 tsp onion powder

2 tsp (12 g) sea salt, divided, plus more if needed

½ tsp black pepper, plus more if needed

2 cups (182 g) chopped broccoli florets

1 cup (146 g) raw unsalted cashews (see Cooking Tips)

2 tbsp (10 g) nutritional yeast

1 tbsp (15 ml) lemon juice

1½ cups (360 ml) water

2 green onions, diced

Set the oven to 400°F (200°C)—no need to preheat. Line a rimmed baking sheet with foil or parchment paper.

Lay the bacon pieces out flat on the baking sheet and cook for 12 to 15 minutes, or until crispy. When the bacon is done, remove the pan from the oven and drain the bacon on a paper towel-lined plate.

While the bacon is cooking, chop the onion, carrots and potatoes. Heat the ghee or olive oil in a large stockpot over medium heat. Add the onion, carrots and garlic. Sauté for 3 to 4 minutes, or until they begin to soften. Add the potatoes, chicken broth, paprika, onion powder, 1 teaspoon of the salt and pepper. Bring to a boil, and then reduce the heat to medium, cover and cook for 10 minutes. Stir in the broccoli and cook for 10 minutes.

With a slotted spoon, remove 1 cup (150 g) of the diced potatoes from the pot and place them into a high-speed blender. Add the cashews, nutritional yeast, lemon juice, remaining salt and water. Blend on high for 1 minute, or until it becomes very thick and creamy. Pour the mixture into the stockpot, and stir well until combined. Taste and add more salt and pepper if needed. Break the bacon into pieces. Serve the soup topped with bacon bits and the green onions.

Cooking Tips: *To avoid using the oven, you can cook the bacon pieces directly in the stockpot while you are chopping the vegetables. Remove the bacon pieces using a slotted spoon and set them aside to drain. Use the rendered bacon fat to sauté the onion, carrots and garlic and omit the cooking oil. This will increase the prep time by 5 minutes.*

To make this vegan, use vegetable broth instead of chicken broth and omit the bacon.

To make this nut free, use 1 cup (240 ml) of full-fat coconut milk in place of the cashews. Reduce the water amount to 1 cup (240 ml).

If you do not have a high-speed blender like a Vitamix, I recommend soaking the cashews for at least 1 hour and then draining them before blending.

Zoodles with Italian Sausage, Fennel and Mushrooms

Egg Free, Low Carb, Nut Free

This "pasta" recipe is the perfect quick weeknight meal that can be customized to fit your preferences. The subtle licorice flavor from the fennel paired with the mushrooms and sausage give this dish incredible flavor. This would be a wonderful meal to serve for guests, as it appears fancy, but it's really simple and easy to throw together! I like to use pre-spiralized zucchini noodles ("zoodles") to save time.

Yield: *3-4 servings*
Hands-On Time: *10 minutes*
Hands-Off Time: *5 minutes*

1 tbsp (15 ml) olive oil

1 lb (454 g) ground Italian sausage

10 oz (283 g) white mushrooms, sliced

1 fennel bulb, diced (save fronds for garnish)

2 cloves garlic, minced

1 tsp Italian seasoning

½ tsp sea salt

¼ tsp crushed red pepper flakes

½ cup (120 ml) chicken broth

½ cup (120 ml) full-fat coconut milk (stir well before measuring)

1 lb (454 g) zoodles

Heat the olive oil in a large pot over medium heat. Add the sausage, mushrooms, fennel and garlic. Cook for 5 to 7 minutes, using a spoon to break up the sausage. Add the Italian seasoning, salt, crushed red pepper flakes and chicken broth. Stir to combine. Cover and let it cook for 5 minutes. Stir, and then add the coconut milk and zoodles. Stir for 2 to 3 minutes, or until the zoodles are softened. Serve with the reserved fennel fronds on top.

30-Minute Turkey and Butternut Squash Chili

Egg Free, Nut Free, Vegan Option

This is a great classic chili recipe that is packed with flavor. I love the sweet butternut squash combined with the cayenne pepper. Raw cacao powder gives this chili an incredibly rich flavor profile. This chili is very easy to make and is also great for feeding a crowd. It freezes and reheats well and makes a wonderful option for meal prep.

Yield: *4–6 servings*

Hands-On Time: *10 minutes*

Hands-Off Time: *20 minutes (minimum), or longer if desired*

1 tbsp (15 ml) olive oil

½ red onion, diced, plus more for serving

1 lb (454 g) ground turkey (see Cooking Tips)

3 cloves garlic, minced

4 cups (560 g) cubed butternut squash (see Cooking Tips)

1 (28-oz [794-g]) can diced tomatoes with juices

1 (15-oz [444-ml]) can tomato sauce

1 (4-oz [113-g]) can fire-roasted diced green chilis

1 cup (240 ml) beef or chicken broth (see Cooking Tips)

1 tbsp (15 ml) coconut aminos

2 tbsp (13 g) chili powder

1 tbsp (8 g) cumin

1 tsp paprika

1 tbsp (5 g) raw cacao powder

1 tsp oregano

1½ tsp (9 g) sea salt

½ tsp black pepper

¼ tsp cayenne pepper (optional)

Fresh cilantro, sliced avocado and sliced jalapeños, for serving (optional)

Heat the olive oil in a large soup pot over medium heat. Add the onion and ground turkey. Cook, using a wooden spoon to break up the turkey, for 5 to 7 minutes, or until the turkey is mostly browned and the onion is beginning to soften. Add the minced garlic and stir for 1 minute. Add the squash, diced tomatoes with their juices, tomato sauce, green chilis, broth, aminos, chili powder, cumin, paprika, cacao powder, oregano, salt, pepper and cayenne pepper (if using). Stir well and bring to a boil, and then reduce the heat to medium-low.

Cover and simmer for a minimum of 20 minutes, or until the butternut squash is fork-tender. You can cook it longer if you want. (The squash will just become more tender.) Serve topped with cilantro, diced red onion, avocado and/or jalapeños, if desired. You can freeze this chili (once cooled) for up to 3 months.

Cooking Tips: *To make this in the Instant Pot, set the Instant Pot to "sauté" mode, and add the olive oil. Cook the onion and ground turkey until mostly browned, and then add the garlic and stir for an additional minute. Press "keep warm/cancel," and add the remaining ingredients (except for the garnishes), plus an extra ½ cup (120 ml) of broth. This will prevent the chili from burning. Stir well, and then lock the lid and turn the vent to "sealing." Press "manual" (check that it's set to high pressure) and set the timer for 15 minutes. Manually release the pressure.*

To make this in the slow cooker, follow the sauté instructions on the stovetop. Add the onion, turkey and garlic to the slow cooker. Add the remaining ingredients and stir well. Cook on low for 7 to 8 hours or high for 3 to 4 hours.

To make this vegan, omit the turkey and beef or chicken broth and replace with vegetables of choice (diced peppers, carrots, etc.) and vegetable broth.

You can find pre-cubed butternut squash in the produce section of most grocery stores. Frozen cubed squash will also work. If peeling and cubing your own butternut squash by hand, be aware this will add to the prep time.

Hearty Cabbage and Kielbasa Soup

Egg Free, Nut Free

This soup reminds me of St. Patrick's Day or a traditional Irish dinner, except in soup form! If you are a meat and potatoes kind of person, this soup will be right up your alley. The kielbasa, potatoes, cabbage and carrots in a savory broth is sure to warm you right up. It also makes great leftovers! Try to look for kielbasa without any sugar to keep it Paleo.

Yield: *6-8 servings*
Hands-On Time: *10 minutes*
Hands-Off Time: *25 minutes*

1 tbsp (15 ml) olive oil

1 onion, diced

13 oz (369 g) sugar-free kielbasa or smoked sausage, cut into rounds

3 cloves garlic, minced

1 small head cabbage, cut into 1-inch (2.5-cm) pieces

3 large carrots, peeled and cut into rounds

3 medium red potatoes, cut into 1-inch (2.5-cm) pieces

1½ tsp (3 g) Italian seasoning

1 tsp sea salt, plus more to taste

1 tsp caraway seeds

½ tsp black pepper, plus more to taste

2 tsp (10 ml) apple cider vinegar

6 cups (1.4 L) chicken broth

Heat the olive oil in a large stockpot or Dutch oven over medium heat. Add the onion and kielbasa. Cook for 3 to 4 minutes, or until the onion is beginning to soften. Add the garlic and stir for 30 seconds until it's fragrant. Add the cabbage, carrots, potatoes, Italian seasoning, salt, caraway seeds, pepper, vinegar and chicken broth, and bring it to a boil. Reduce the heat to a simmer and let the soup cook for 20 to 25 minutes, or until the potatoes and carrots are tender. Season with salt and pepper to taste.

Perfect Dutch Oven Roasted Chicken

Egg Free, Nut Free

Roasting an entire chicken always used to intimidate me until I realized how incredibly simple (and foolproof) it can be! Coating the chicken in a lemony garlic ghee mixture before roasting gives it the crispiest skin every single time. The carrots, onion and sweet potato get cooked in the juices from the chicken, which gives them the most irresistible savory flavor. Feel free to use whatever potatoes or vegetables you have on hand, or omit them completely. If you don't have a Dutch oven, you can simply use a regular roasting pan. And be sure to save your chicken bones to make your own bone broth! To save time, use pre-minced garlic, pre-chopped sweet potatoes and pre-chopped carrots.

Yield: *3-4 servings*

Hands-On Time: *10 minutes*

Hands-Off Time: *1½ hours (this may vary depending on the size of your chicken)*

4-5-lb (1.8-2.3-kg) roasting chicken, giblets and neck removed

1 tbsp (15 ml) olive oil

1 large onion, quartered, divided

2 cups (268 g) diced sweet potatoes (see Cooking Tips)

1 lb (454 g) petit tricolor carrots (or regular carrots cut into ½-inch [1.3-cm]-long slices, see Cooking Tips)

2 tbsp (30 ml) melted ghee

½ lemon, juiced and reserved

2 cloves garlic, minced

1 tsp sea salt

½ tsp black pepper

1 sprig rosemary

3 sprigs thyme

3 sage leaves

Preheat the oven to 425°F (220°C). Pat the chicken dry and set aside.

Add the olive oil to a medium-sized (5-quart [5-L]) Dutch oven along with 2 of the onion quarters (separated into smaller pieces), the sweet potatoes and the carrots.

In a small bowl, add the ghee, lemon juice, garlic, salt and pepper and mix well. Stuff the remaining onion quarters, the squeezed lemon half, the rosemary, thyme and sage into the cavity of the chicken. Pour the ghee mixture over the top and use your hands to spread it all over the chicken, making sure to get in every crevice. Roast for 1½ hours, or until the internal temperature of the thickest part of the chicken reaches 165°F (75°C).

Cooking Tips: *You can use any type of potato or root vegetable in the pot. Alternatively, you can roast the vegetables separately if you prefer them to be crispier. Just add them to a parchment paper-lined baking sheet and roast in the oven for the last 30 minutes of the chicken's cooking time.*

Unstuffed Pepper Soup

Egg Free, Low Carb, Nut Free

This soup has all of the flavors of stuffed peppers with one-quarter of the effort!
It's loaded with ground beef, Italian spices, tomatoes and cauliflower rice to keep it grain free.
I prefer to use frozen cauliflower rice instead of fresh because it has a better texture. This soup
is a great low-carb option, and it makes incredible leftovers!

Yield: *4-6 servings*
Hands-On Time: *10 minutes*
Hands-Off Time: *30 minutes*

1 tbsp (15 ml) olive oil

½ medium onion, diced

1 lb (454 g) ground beef (see
Cooking Tips)

2 cloves garlic, minced

1 red bell pepper, diced

1 green bell pepper, diced

1 (16-oz [454-g]) bag frozen
cauliflower rice

1 tsp oregano

1 tsp thyme

1 (14.5-oz [411-g]) can diced tomatoes
with juices

1 (15-oz [444-ml]) can tomato sauce

3 cups (720 ml) sugar-free beef broth

1½ tsp (9 g) sea salt

Chopped parsley, for serving (optional)

Heat the olive oil in a large stockpot over medium heat. Add the onion, ground beef and garlic. Sauté for 5 to 7 minutes, or until the beef is browned and the onion is translucent. Add the bell peppers, cauliflower rice, oregano, thyme, diced tomatoes, tomato sauce, beef broth and salt. Stir everything to combine.

Bring to a boil, and then reduce the heat to medium-low and simmer for 30 minutes, or until the peppers are softened. Serve with chopped parsley, if desired.

Cooking Tips: *To make this in the Instant Pot, set the Instant Pot to "sauté" mode and heat the olive oil. Add the onion, ground beef and garlic and cook for 5 to 7 minutes. Add the remaining ingredients (except for the garnishes). Lock the lid, turn the vent to "sealing," press "manual" (check that it's set to high pressure) and set the timer for 10 minutes. Manually release the pressure and stir.*

To make this in the slow cooker, sauté the onion, ground beef and garlic in a pan before transferring to the slow cooker. Add the remaining ingredients (except for the garnish) and cook on low for 8 to 10 hours or high for 4 to 5 hours.

You can also use ground pork, turkey or chicken instead of ground beef.

Quick Creamy Bolognese Sauce

Egg Free, Low Carb, Nut-Free Option

Traditional Bolognese sauce, or ragu, is slow-cooked and sometimes made with milk or heavy cream. This lightened-up version comes together in just 20 minutes from start to finish and pairs perfectly with any type of vegetable noodle. Stirring in a cashew cream sauce at the end gives it a delicious richness without any of the dairy. You can let the sauce cook for up to 4 hours before adding the cashew cream. Also, replacing half of the ground beef with ground pork gives this sauce great flavor! I like to serve this with Perfect Roasted Spaghetti Squash (page 169) or zucchini noodles.

Yield: *4-6 servings*
Hands-On Time: *10 minutes*
Hands-Off Time: *10 minutes*

1 tbsp (15 ml) olive oil

½ onion, diced

2 large carrots, peeled and diced

2 ribs celery, diced

2 cloves garlic, minced

1 lb (454 g) ground beef

3 cups (720 ml) marinara sauce (I like Rao's Homemade brand)

1 tsp Italian seasoning

1 bay leaf

1 tsp sea salt

½ cup (73 g) raw, unsalted cashews (see Cooking Tips)

¾ cup (180 ml) water

Chopped parsley, for serving (optional)

Heat the olive oil in a large Dutch oven or stockpot over medium heat. Add the onion, carrots, celery and garlic. Sauté for 2 to 3 minutes. Add the ground beef and stir until browned but not fully cooked through, approximately 5 minutes. Add the marinara sauce, Italian seasoning, bay leaf and salt. Stir, cover and let cook over medium-low heat while you make the cashew cream sauce.

For the cashew cream, combine the cashews and water in a high-speed blender, and blend for at least 1 minute on high. It should be very creamy with no chunks. Stir the cashew cream into the sauce and serve with chopped parsley, if desired. Remove the bay leaf before serving.

Cooking Tips: *Omit the cashew cream for a nut-free sauce, or alternatively, you can stir in ½ cup (120 ml) of coconut cream.*

If you do not have a high-speed blender like a Vitamix, I recommend soaking the cashews for at least 1 hour and then draining them before blending.

Grain-Free Jambalaya

Egg Free, Low Carb, Nut Free

Traditional jambalaya is usually made with vegetables, various types of sausage, seafood and rice. I used a combination of andouille sausage and shrimp here with the option to add pre-cooked chicken, as well as cauliflower rice to keep it grain free. This dish is loaded with Creole spices and definitely packs some heat. This is pure comfort food that you can prep in less than 10 minutes before you pop it in the oven.

Yield: *4-6 servings*
Hands-On Time: *10 minutes*
Hands-Off Time: *50-60 minutes*

1 tbsp (15 ml) olive oil or avocado oil

1 medium onion, diced

1 green bell pepper, diced

2 cloves garlic, minced

1 lb (454 g) frozen shrimp (pre-peeled, deveined and tails removed)

1 lb (454 g) smoked sausage or andouille sausage, cut into ¼-inch (6-mm) rounds

1 (16-oz [454-g]) bag frozen cauliflower rice

1 (28-oz [794-g]) can chopped tomatoes

1 tsp dried oregano

1 tsp paprika

½ tsp dried thyme

½ tsp crushed red pepper flakes (optional)

¼ tsp cayenne pepper (optional)

1½ tsp (9 g) sea salt

Chopped green onions, for serving (optional)

Preheat the oven to 375°F (190°C).

Heat the oil in a large Dutch oven or skillet over medium heat. Add the onion, bell pepper and garlic. Stir for 3 to 4 minutes, or until the onion and bell pepper begin to soften and the garlic is fragrant. If using a Dutch oven, add the shrimp, sausage, cauliflower rice, chopped tomatoes, oregano, paprika, thyme, crushed red pepper flakes (if using), cayenne pepper (if using) and salt. Or, if you don't have a Dutch oven, transfer the onion, bell pepper and garlic to a 9 x 12-inch (23 x 30-cm) oven-safe casserole dish and add the remaining ingredients.

Stir everything together. Bake for 45 to 50 minutes, stirring halfway through, until the shrimp are pink and cooked through and the jambalaya is bubbling around the edges. Serve topped with chopped green onions, if desired.

Cooking Tip: *You can also add 2 cups (250 g) of pre-cooked, shredded chicken to the mix before baking.*

15-Minute (Or Less)
Masterpieces

All of the recipes in this chapter are designed to be prepped AND cooked in less than 15 minutes. These meals are perfect for busy weeknights or making for a quick grab-and-go lunch. My hope is that this chapter will give you inspiration for making meals using fresh Paleo ingredients like ground beef/pork, veggies, eggs and seafood without having to spend more than 15 minutes in the kitchen!

Some of these recipes do not involve any cooking, like Moroccan Chicken Salad (page 101), Cilantro-Lime Tuna-Stuffed Avocados (page 105) and the Crab Stack Salad (page 114), which are great for summer or days when you don't want to turn your stovetop or oven on! They also work well for taking to work and having a quick lunch that doesn't require a microwave.

My favorite recipe in this chapter is the Bell Pepper Nachos with Simple Weeknight Taco Meat (page 113) because it is so versatile. You can easily use this taco meat for tacos, bowls, lettuce wraps or the bell pepper nachos as suggested.

Deconstructed Burger Bowl
with Special Sauce

Egg-Free Option, Low Carb, Nut Free

This super quick and easy burger bowl tastes exactly like a juicy Big Mac, except without
a bun or the dairy! This recipe is totally customizable, and you can use whatever toppings you like.
I love adding bacon, but it is definitely optional. To make this for meal prep, store the ground beef
and bacon separately and create bowls throughout the week.

Yield: *3 bowls*
Hands–On Time: *10 minutes*
Hands–Off Time: *none*

For the Ground Beef

1 tbsp (15 ml) olive oil

1 lb (454 g) ground beef

½ tsp sea salt

½ tsp garlic powder

½ tsp onion powder

For the Special Sauce

¼ cup (60 ml) mayonnaise (see
Cooking Tips)

2 tbsp (30 ml) ketchup

1 tbsp (15 ml) Dijon mustard

1 tsp hot sauce

1 tsp coconut aminos

Suggested Bowl Accompaniments

6 pieces bacon, cooked (see
Cooking Tips)

Grape tomatoes

Lettuce

Red onions

Avocado

Pickles

To make the ground beef, heat the olive oil in a large skillet over medium heat. Add
the ground beef, salt, garlic powder and onion powder, and cook for 5 to 7 minutes,
or until cooked through, using a spoon to break up the meat. Drain any fat from
the pan.

While the beef is cooking, make the special sauce by mixing the mayonnaise,
ketchup, mustard, hot sauce and coconut aminos in a small bowl.

Serve the ground beef in a bowl with the suggested accompaniments and special
sauce. You can store the ground beef and the special sauce in the refrigerator for
up to 4 days.

Cooking Tips: *To make this egg free, substitute vegan mayonnaise for the
regular mayonnaise.*

*To cook bacon without making a mess, simply lay the bacon pieces on a foil-
lined baking sheet without overlapping them. Bake at 400°F (200°C) for 13 to
15 minutes, or until your desired level of crispiness has been reached. Drain
the pieces on a paper towel-lined plate.*

Moroccan Chicken Salad

Nut-Free Option, Egg-Free Option

The key, in my opinion, to making the perfect chicken salad is having a little bit of sweetness with a bit of crunch. This unique version combines shredded chicken with mayo, Moroccan spices (like cinnamon, cumin and coriander), dried fruits (like raisins and apricots) and sliced almonds. It's delicious served on Bibb lettuce leaves, on grain-free tortillas, on top of a bed of greens or simply on its own!

Yield: *3-4 servings*

Hands-On Time: *10 minutes*

Hands-Off Time: *none*

3 cups (375 g) cooked shredded chicken (approximately 1½ lbs [680 g] chicken breasts, see Cooking Tips)

½ cup (120 ml) mayonnaise (see Cooking Tips)

2 tbsp (2 g) chopped fresh cilantro

10 dried apricots, finely chopped

⅓ cup (48 g) raisins

⅓ cup (36 g) sliced almonds (see Cooking Tips)

½ tbsp (8 ml) lemon juice

1 tsp cinnamon

½ tsp cumin

½ tsp ground ginger

½ tsp paprika

½ tsp sea salt

¼ tsp coriander

Bibb or butter lettuce leaves or grain-free tortillas, for serving (optional)

In a large bowl, mix the chicken, mayonnaise, cilantro, apricots, raisins, almonds, lemon juice, cinnamon, cumin, ginger, paprika, salt and coriander. Serve in lettuce cups or in grain-free tortillas. This chicken salad can be stored in the refrigerator for up to 4 days.

Cooking Tips: *If using rotisserie chicken, be sure to read the label. Many of them contain non-Paleo ingredients.*

To quickly make chicken breasts for shredding, bring 1½ pounds (680 g) of chicken breasts to a boil in a pot of water. Once boiling, cover the pot and remove it from the heat. Let it sit for 15 minutes, and then remove the chicken breasts and shred them using two forks.

To make this egg free, substitute vegan mayonnaise for the regular mayonnaise.

Omit the almonds for a nut-free version.

Asparagus and Mushroom "Risotto"

Egg Free, Low Carb, Vegan Option

Risotto is typically made using arborio rice that is cooked in broth while constantly stirring until it reaches a creamy consistency. This quicker Paleo version uses frozen cauliflower rice and a cashew cream with broth, and it is unbelievable how much it tastes like the real thing! You can pair it with your protein of choice, or enjoy it as-is for a delicious vegetarian meal.

Yield: *3-4 servings*
Hands-On Time: *15 minutes*
Hands-Off Time: *none*

2 tbsp (24 g) ghee (see Cooking Tips)

1 shallot, diced

2 cloves garlic, minced

8 oz (226 g) baby Bella mushrooms, sliced

8 oz (226 g) asparagus, cut into 1-2-inch (2.5-5-cm) pieces

1 (16-oz [454-g]) bag frozen cauliflower rice

¾ cup (180 ml) chicken broth (see Cooking Tips)

1 tsp sea salt

¼ tsp black pepper

¾ cup (109 g) raw, unsalted cashews (see Cooking Tips)

1 cup (240 ml) water

Crumbled cooked bacon, for serving (optional)

Heat the ghee in a large nonstick skillet over medium heat. Add the shallot, garlic, mushrooms and asparagus. Sauté for 3 to 4 minutes, or until the garlic is fragrant and the vegetables are beginning to soften. Add the frozen cauliflower rice, chicken broth, salt and pepper. Stir well, and then cover. Let it cook over medium heat while you make the cashew cream.

Add the cashews and water to a high-speed blender and blend on high for 1 minute, or until very creamy. There should be no lumps or visible pieces of cashew. Scrape down the sides halfway through, blending if needed. Pour the cashew cream into the skillet and stir well. There will be a lot of liquid, but it will thicken and some of it will cook off quickly. Continue stirring every 1 to 2 minutes for about 5 minutes, or until the desired consistency is reached. Top with crumbled bacon, if desired.

Cooking Tips: *To make this vegan, use vegetable broth instead of chicken broth, and coconut oil instead of ghee. Omit the optional bacon.*

If you do not have a high-speed blender like a Vitamix, I recommend soaking the cashews for at least 1 hour and then draining them before blending.

Cilantro-Lime Tuna-Stuffed Avocados

Low Carb, Nut Free, Egg-Free Option

This is a great quick meal that packs in a lot of protein and healthy fats without taking up a ton of time in the kitchen. I always have canned tuna in the pantry, so these can be whipped together in no time. I like to keep avocados in my refrigerator as this helps them last longer and ripen slower. The cilantro and lime juice give this tuna a unique Southwest flavor and pair so well with the creamy avocado!

Yield: *4 stuffed avocados*
Hands-On Time: *10 minutes*
Hands-Off Time: *none*

2 (5-oz [142-g]) cans tuna

2 tbsp (20 g) diced red onion

2 ribs celery, diced

1½ tbsp (23 ml) mayonnaise (or more if you like it creamier, see Cooking Tip)

1 tbsp (15 ml) hot sauce (I like Frank's RedHot)

1 tbsp (1 g) chopped fresh cilantro, plus extra for serving

1 tbsp (15 ml) lime juice, plus extra for serving

¼ tsp sea salt

2 large avocados

In a large bowl, combine the tuna, onion, celery, mayonnaise, hot sauce, cilantro, lime juice and salt. Mash with a fork. Cut the avocados in half lengthwise and remove the pits. Leave the skin on. Fill each avocado half with a generous scoop of the tuna salad. Top with an extra squeeze of lime and more chopped cilantro, if desired. These can be covered and stored in the refrigerator for up to 3 days.

Cooking Tip: *To make this egg free, substitute vegan mayonnaise for the regular mayonnaise.*

Spicy Shrimp Lettuce Wraps with Mango Salsa

Egg Free, Low Carb, Nut Free

I love having frozen shrimp on hand for busy weeknights when I don't have a dinner plan. They can be thawed quickly in a colander under cold running water and cooked up quickly. It's also important to look for shrimp that have already been peeled and deveined, as this will save a bunch of time. These lettuce wraps are the perfect combination of sweet and spicy, and they are so fresh and delicious.

Yield: *3–4 servings*
Hands–On Time: *10 minutes*
Hands–Off Time: *none*

For the Mango Salsa

2 cups (330 g) finely diced mango

½ cup (80 g) diced red onion

1 cup (149 g) diced red bell pepper

1 jalapeño, deseeded and diced

2 tbsp (30 ml) lime juice

¼ cup (4 g) chopped cilantro

¼ tsp sea salt

For the Shrimp

1 tbsp (15 ml) olive oil or avocado oil

1 lb (454 g) fresh or frozen and thawed shrimp (pre-peeled, deveined and tails removed)

1 tsp paprika

½ tsp crushed red pepper flakes

½ tsp garlic powder

¼ tsp sea salt

For Serving

1 head butter lettuce

To make the salsa, in a large bowl, mix together the mango, onion, red bell pepper, jalapeño, lime juice, cilantro and salt. Refrigerate until ready to serve.

To make the shrimp, heat the oil in a large skillet over medium heat. Add the shrimp, paprika, crushed red pepper flakes, garlic powder and salt. Cook the shrimp for 2 minutes per side, until cooked through and no longer translucent. Serve 2 to 3 shrimp in each butter lettuce leaf, and top with the mango salsa. You can make the salsa up to 2 days ahead of time, and it can be stored in the refrigerator for up to 4 days.

Deviled Egg Salad Endive Cups

Low Carb, Nut Free, Vegetarian Option

This classic egg salad recipe combines bacon, chives, mayo and Dijon mustard and is made faster by using store-bought boiled eggs. It tastes just like deviled eggs without the hassle of making and filling them! Endive is a leaf vegetable that has a crunchy texture and a pleasant, mild bitterness. The leaves make a great vessel for this egg salad (I promise you won't even miss the bread). This would make a delicious lunch or even breakfast. Make this recipe even easier by making the bacon ahead of time and storing it in the refrigerator until you're ready to use it.

Yield: *3-4 servings*
Hands-On Time: *15 minutes*
Hands-Off Time: *none*

4 strips sugar-free bacon (see Cooking Tips)

8 large hard-boiled eggs (see Cooking Tips)

3 tbsp (45 ml) mayonnaise (I like Sir Kensington's brand)

¼ cup (4 g) diced chives

2 tsp (10 ml) Dijon mustard

¼ tsp sea salt

¼ tsp black pepper

1 tbsp (15 ml) hot sauce

12-15 endive leaves (depending on their size)

Set the oven to 400°F (200°C)—no need to preheat. Line a rimmed baking sheet with foil or parchment paper.

Lay the bacon pieces out flat on the baking sheet and cook for 12 to 15 minutes, or until crispy. When the bacon is done, remove the pan from the oven and drain the bacon on a paper towel-lined plate. Crumble the bacon into pieces.

Finely chop the hard-boiled eggs and add them to a large bowl. Add the mayonnaise, chives, mustard, salt, pepper and hot sauce and mix well. Add the bacon pieces and stir. Tear off the endive leaves and fill each one with a scoop of the egg salad. This egg salad can be stored in an airtight container in the refrigerator for up to 4 days.

Cooking Tips: *Omit the bacon to make this recipe vegetarian.*

To quickly make hard-boiled eggs in the Instant Pot, place the trivet in the bottom of the pot and pour in 1 cup (240 ml) of water. Place the eggs on top of the trivet and lock the lid. Turn the vent to "sealing." Press "manual" (check that it's set to high pressure) and set the timer for 7 minutes. Manually release the pressure and then transfer the eggs to an ice bath to halt cooking. Peel and dice!

Pineapple Pork Fried "Rice"

Egg-Free Option, Nut Free

Chinese takeout used to happen often around here. Unfortunately, a lot of it is filled with MSG, gluten and other stuff that doesn't make me feel so great. Luckily you can still have all of the delicious flavors of your favorite fried rice with this Paleo version! The pineapple gives it a sweetness that really complements the pork. The addition of coleslaw mix plus riced cauliflower gives it a nice texture, while still keeping it low carb. The egg is optional, but delicious if you can tolerate eggs!

Yield: 4-6 servings
Hands-On Time: 10 minutes
Hands-Off Time: 5 minutes

1 lb (454 g) ground pork (see Cooking Tip)

1 cup (70 g) diced mushrooms

½ red onion, diced

1 cup (165 g) finely diced and drained canned pineapple chunks or drained crushed pineapple

2 cloves garlic, minced

1 (16-oz [454-g]) bag cauliflower rice

1 (14-oz [397-g]) bag coleslaw mix

1 tsp ground ginger

½ cup (120 ml) coconut aminos

1 tsp rice vinegar

1 tsp toasted sesame oil

1 tsp sea salt

1 large egg (optional)

Chopped green onions, for serving (optional)

Heat a large skillet over medium heat. Add the pork (no oil necessary), and cook for 3 to 4 minutes, using a spoon to break it up. While the pork is browning, chop the mushrooms, onion and pineapple (if using chunks). Add the onion, mushrooms and garlic to the pan and stir for 2 to 3 minutes. Add the cauliflower rice, coleslaw, pineapple, ginger, aminos, rice vinegar, sesame oil and salt, and stir well. Cover the pan and let it cook for 3 to 4 minutes. Stir.

If adding the egg, scramble it in a separate pan while everything else is cooking. Add the scrambled egg to the large pan and stir to combine with everything else. Serve topped with green onions. This can be stored in the refrigerator for up to 4 days.

Cooking Tip: *You can also use ground chicken, ground beef or ground turkey in this recipe. If using chicken or turkey, add 1 tablespoon (15 ml) of olive oil before sautéing it.*

Bell Pepper Nachos with Simple Weeknight Taco Meat

Egg Free, Low Carb, Nut Free

Bell pepper "nachos" are a fun, low-carb way to eat Mexican food while incorporating more vegetables into your diet. Sliced bell peppers are topped with my go-to weeknight taco meat mixture, avocado, black olives, jalapeños and cilantro. You can feel free to get creative with these and add any topping you want! Grain-free chips can also replace the bell peppers. You can also use ground chicken or ground turkey for this recipe. The simple weeknight taco meat is also delicious in tacos, salads and bowls.

Yield: *3-4 servings*
Hands–On Time: *10 minutes*
Hands–Off Time: *5 minutes*

2 bell peppers (any color), cut into 2-inch (5-cm) pieces

1 lb (454 g) ground beef

2 tsp (5 g) chili powder

1 tsp cumin

½ tsp sea salt

½ tsp paprika

½ tsp oregano

½ tsp onion powder

½ tsp garlic powder

Dash of cayenne pepper (optional)

1 (8-oz [226-g]) can tomato sauce

Options for Serving
Diced avocado

Cilantro

Black olives

Sliced jalapeños

Place the bell pepper pieces on a large plate or tray. Set aside.

Heat a large skillet over medium heat. Add the ground beef, chili powder, cumin, salt, paprika, oregano, onion powder, garlic powder and cayenne (if using). Cook for 5 to 7 minutes, using a wooden spoon to break the meat up into pieces. Add the tomato sauce and stir. Let it simmer for 3 to 4 minutes on medium-low heat until the sauce has thickened. Spoon some of the taco meat onto each bell pepper and add the avocado, cilantro, black olives and/or sliced jalapeños.

Crab Stack Salad

Egg Free, Low Carb, Nut Free

During a recent dinner at a popular upscale steakhouse, my husband and I split a "crab stack," which consisted of jumbo lump crabmeat, mango, avocado and red bell peppers in a light vinaigrette. They called it a stack because it was in a perfect cylindrical form—almost too pretty to eat! I decided to make my own deconstructed version using a few simple Paleo ingredients, which can be thrown together in almost no time at all. This salad can be served over greens or eaten by itself. It could also be used as a salsa on top of fish or eaten with some grain-free chips! I would not recommend using canned crabmeat or fake crabmeat for this recipe. Fresh jumbo lump or lump meat is preferred.

Yield: *3-4 servings*
Hands-On Time: *10 minutes*
Hands-Off Time: *none*

8 oz (226 g) jumbo lump crabmeat (fresh is preferred, see Cooking Tip)

1 cup (149 g) diced red bell pepper

1 cup (150 g) diced avocado

1 cup (165 g) diced mango

¼ cup (40 g) finely diced red onion

1 tbsp (1 g) finely diced fresh cilantro

1 clove garlic, minced

1 tbsp (15 ml) Dijon mustard

¼ cup (60 ml) olive oil

2 tsp (10 ml) red wine vinegar

2 tbsp (30 ml) lime juice

¼ tsp sea salt, plus more to taste

Black pepper, to taste

Place the crabmeat, bell pepper, avocado, mango, onion and cilantro in a large bowl. Set aside. In a small dish, whisk the garlic, mustard, olive oil, red wine vinegar, lime juice and salt . Pour the mixture over the crabmeat and use a spatula to lightly toss it all together. Add more salt and pepper, to taste.

Cooking Tip: *You could also make this recipe using ½ pound (226 g) of chopped, cooked shrimp.*

Comforting
Casseroles

Casseroles are the ultimate form of comfort food in my opinion. I've provided a variety of comforting dishes in this chapter that taste decadent but are made with alternative ingredients to keep them dairy free and gluten free. They are also easy to whip up for dinner on a busy weeknight or can be prepped ahead of time and baked later. All of the casseroles in this chapter make excellent leftovers, so you can make them on a Sunday and easily reheat them for lunches or dinners throughout the week. Most of these casseroles take about 15 minutes to prepare because there are usually multiple moving parts like making the sauce, browning the meat, etc.

Some low-carb casserole options in this chapter include Spinach-Artichoke Chicken Casserole (page 118) and Chicken Bacon Ranch Casserole (page 126). Meanwhile, the Chicken Cordon Bleu Bake (page 122), Jalapeño Tuna "Noodle" Casserole (page 130) and the "Cheese"-Burger Casserole (page 129) are all made using a cashew cream sauce, which is an incredibly rich and creamy alternative to dairy.

If you're looking for some nut-free options, the Loaded Sweet Potato Taco Casserole (page 121), Spinach-Artichoke Chicken Casserole (page 118) and Meat Lovers' Pizza Spaghetti Squash Casserole (page 125) are all great choices!

Spinach-Artichoke Chicken Casserole

Low Carb, Nut Free

Any other spinach-artichoke dip fans out there? It used to be my go-to appetizer to order (or make) on game day. I wanted to create a complete meal that utilized a dairy-free version of this creamy dip with a protein and some extra veggies. Enter this simple and cozy casserole! The nutritional yeast gives it a cheesy flavor without the dairy. The leftovers heat up nicely as well! You can make the sauce up to 2 days in advance to save time.

Yield: *4-6 servings*

Hands-On Time: *10 minutes*

Hands-Off Time: *35-40 minutes*

1 tbsp (12 g) ghee or 1 tbsp (15 ml) cooking oil, plus extra for greasing

2 large chicken breasts, sliced in half to make 4 thinner breasts (see Cooking Tip)

2 tsp (12 g) sea salt, divided

½ tsp black pepper

3 cups (90 g) tightly packed raw spinach, chopped

1 (28-oz [794-g]) can artichoke hearts, drained and chopped

1 (16-oz [454-g]) bag frozen cauliflower rice

1¼ cups (300 ml) mayonnaise

½ cup (120 ml) full-fat coconut milk (stir well before measuring)

3 cloves garlic, minced

¼ cup (20 g) nutritional yeast

1 tsp onion powder

1 tbsp (15 ml) lemon juice

1 tbsp (15 ml) Dijon mustard

Preheat the oven to 350°F (180°C). Lightly grease a 9 x 13-inch (23 x 33-cm) casserole dish with ghee or cooking oil.

Heat the ghee or cooking oil in a large skillet. Season the chicken breasts with 1 teaspoon of the salt and the pepper, and then cook for 2 to 3 minutes per side until browned but not cooked through. Remove the chicken breasts from the pan and set aside. While the chicken is browning, chop the spinach and artichokes. Add them to the casserole dish along with the frozen cauliflower rice.

In a large bowl, mix the mayonnaise, coconut milk, garlic, nutritional yeast, onion powder, lemon juice, Dijon mustard and remaining salt. Pour the sauce over the spinach, artichokes and cauliflower rice, reserving ¼ cup (60 ml) for the chicken breasts. Mix well. Place the chicken breasts on top of the mixture and press down slightly. Pour the remaining sauce over the chicken. Bake for 35 to 40 minutes, or until the sides of the casserole are bubbling and the chicken is cooked through. Serve the chicken on top of the cauliflower rice and artichoke mixture.

Cooking Tip: *To make this using pre-cooked chicken, simply add 3 cups (375 g) of shredded or chopped chicken to the casserole dish with the spinach, artichokes and cauliflower rice. Pour the sauce over the top. Mix well and bake for 30 minutes, until bubbling and heated through.*

Loaded Sweet Potato Taco Casserole

My family loves this casserole, which combines taco meat, veggies, sweet potatoes and a creamy mixture of salsa and mayo to hold it all together. It is simple and versatile—top it with some jalapeños, tomatoes, avocado, cilantro and lime juice and you've got yourself the perfect weeknight meal. The leftovers are amazing with an egg on top for breakfast too!

Yield: *4–6 servings*
Hands-On Time: *10 minutes*
Hands-Off Time: *35 minutes*

Avocado or olive oil cooking spray

1 tbsp (15 ml) olive oil or avocado oil

1 lb (454 g) ground beef

1 bell pepper (any color), deseeded and diced

1 onion, diced

1 large sweet potato, diced (about 3 cups [402 g])

2 tsp (5 g) chili powder

1 tsp cumin

1 tsp sea salt

1 tsp garlic powder

1 tsp onion powder

½ tsp paprika

½ tsp oregano

2 tbsp (30 ml) water

1 (15.5-oz [439-g]) jar salsa

Pinch of cayenne pepper (omit if you don't like it hot)

¾ cup (180 ml) mayonnaise

Juice from 1 lime, plus more if needed

Options for Serving

Jalapeño slices

Avocado slices

Diced tomatoes

Fresh cilantro

Preheat the oven to 400°F (200°C). Spray a 9 x 13-inch (23 x 33-cm) casserole dish with the avocado or olive oil.

Heat the oil in a large skillet over medium heat. Add the ground beef and cook for 3 to 4 minutes, using a spoon to break it up into pieces.

While the beef is browning, chop up the bell pepper, onion and sweet potato. Add the sweet potato to the casserole dish.

Add the onion, bell pepper, chili powder, cumin, salt, garlic powder, onion powder, paprika, oregano and water to the skillet with the beef. Stir for 2 to 3 minutes, or until the onion begins to soften. Pour in the salsa and stir to combine. Pour the beef mixture into the casserole dish. Add the cayenne pepper, mayonnaise and the lime juice and stir everything together. Bake for 35 minutes, or until the top is browned and the edges are crispy. Top with more lime juice, jalapeño slices, avocado slices, diced tomatoes and/or cilantro. You can store this casserole in the refrigerator for up to 4 days.

Cooking Tip: *To save time, chop the sweet potato and make the beef, onion, bell peppers, taco seasoning and salsa mixture ahead of time. Then combine everything together with the mayo and lime juice when you're ready to bake it!*

Chicken Cordon Bleu Bake

✦ Egg Free ✦

Traditional cordon bleu involves rolling up chicken with ham and Swiss cheese stuffed inside,
which is then breaded and topping with a dairy-filled cheesy mustard sauce. To make this Paleo, I decided to
make it in casserole form with tender chunks of chicken, potatoes, ham and a cashew cream "cheese" sauce,
and then I top it off with some grain-free pork panko as the "breading." I can't even believe
how much this tastes like the real thing!

Yield: *4–6 servings*

Hands–On Time: *10 minutes*

Hands–Off Time: *55 minutes*

For the Meat and Potatoes

1½ lbs (680 g) baby potatoes, cut into 1–2-inch (2.5–5-cm) pieces

2 tbsp (30 ml) olive oil

1 tsp sea salt, divided

1 (7-oz [198-g]) package deli ham, chopped into 1-inch (2.5-cm) pieces (I like Applegate brand)

1½ lbs (680 g) chicken breasts, cut into 1–2-inch (2.5–5-cm) pieces

1 cup (56 g) homemade or store-bought pork panko (see Cooking Tips)

For the Cashew "Cheese" Sauce

1½ cups (219 g) raw, unsalted cashews

1 cup (240 ml) chicken broth

2 tbsp (10 g) nutritional yeast

1 tbsp (15 ml) lemon juice

1 tbsp (15 ml) Dijon mustard

1 tsp garlic powder

½ tsp sea salt

For Serving

Parsley (optional)

Preheat the oven to 425°F (220°C).

To make the meat and potatoes, place the potatoes into a 9 x 13-inch (23 x 33-cm) casserole dish, and drizzle with the olive oil and sprinkle with ½ teaspoon of the salt. Toss to coat the potatoes, and then bake for 30 minutes. Toss the potatoes halfway through the cooking time.

While the potatoes are cooking, dice the ham and chicken. Set them aside in the refrigerator while you wait.

To make the cashew "cheese" sauce, place the cashews, chicken broth, nutritional yeast, lemon juice, mustard, garlic powder and salt in a high-speed blender. Blend on high for at least 1 minute, or until the sauce is very creamy and smooth.

When the potatoes come out of the oven, add the raw chicken pieces, followed by the ham. Pour the sauce over top and use a spatula to evenly spread it out and mix it in with the chicken and ham. Sprinkle the pork panko and the remaining salt evenly over the top. Bake the casserole for 25 minutes, or until the chicken reaches an internal temperature of at least 165°F (75°C). Serve with parsley, if desired.

Cooking Tips: *Pork panko is available in many stores and online. If you prefer, you can make your own by crushing up pork rinds. Look for a brand where the ingredients are just pork and sea salt. (Epic brand Oven Baked Pork Rinds are great!)*

If you do not have a high-speed blender like a Vitamix, I recommend soaking the cashews for at least 1 hour and then draining them before blending.

Meat Lovers' Pizza Spaghetti Squash Casserole

Egg Free, Nut-Free Option

This casserole is as close as it gets to eating a big slice of pizza with all the meats, except it's completely gluten free, grain free and dairy free! The spaghetti squash noodles get baked with a combination of Italian sausage and pancetta, marinara sauce and almond milk cream cheese, and then topped with pepperoni. This casserole is totally customizable, and you can add in whatever "pizza" toppings you would like! It's very kid-friendly and perfect for serving to a group. Save time by making the spaghetti squash ahead of time.

Yield: *4-6 servings*
Hands-On Time: *15 minutes*
Hands-Off Time: *1 hour*

Avocado or olive oil cooking spray

1 (4-5-lb [1.8-2.3-kg]) spaghetti squash (or 2 smaller ones)

1½ lbs (680 g) Italian sausage, casings removed

3 oz (85 g) diced pancetta

½ onion, diced

3 cups (720 ml) marinara sauce (I like Rao's Homemade brand)

1 tsp garlic powder

4 oz (113 g) almond milk cream cheese (I like Kite Hill brand, see Cooking Tip)

12 slices pepperoni

Preheat the oven to 400°F (200°C). Line a baking sheet with parchment paper. Lightly spray a 9 x 13-inch (23 x 33-cm) casserole dish with the avocado or olive oil.

Cut the spaghetti squash in half and scoop out the seeds. Place the halves cut side down on the baking sheet. Roast for 35 minutes.

Heat a large skillet over medium heat and add the Italian sausage, pancetta and onion. (You shouldn't need any oil since the sausage will produce its own fat.) Sauté for 5 minutes, or until the sausage is cooked through and the onion is softened. Drain any fat out of the pan. Pour in the marinara sauce, add the garlic power and stir to combine.

When the squash is done, scrape the "noodles" out of each half and add them to the skillet. Stir to combine.

Turn the oven temperature to 375°F (190°C). Add half of the mixture to the bottom of the casserole dish, and use a spatula to spread it out evenly. Add small dots of the cream cheese all over the top of the mixture. Add the rest of the mixture on top of the cream cheese and smooth it out. Add the pepperoni slices to the top, and bake for 25 minutes, or until the sides are bubbling.

Cooking Tip: *To make this nut free, omit the almond milk cream cheese and instead add 1 tablespoon (5 g) of nutritional yeast to the marinara sauce.*

Chicken Bacon Ranch Casserole

Low Carb, Nut Free

In this simple casserole, ground chicken is combined with broccoli, cauliflower rice and ranch dressing. It's baked to perfection and then topped with crispy bacon. It is perfect for meal prepping, as it heats up beautifully. You can also use ground turkey for this recipe. For the ranch dressing, it is important to look for a Paleo brand (I like Tessemae's). Save time by making the bacon ahead of time.

Yield: *4–6 servings*
Hands-On Time: *15 minutes*
Hands-Off Time: *30 minutes*

1 lb (454 g) sugar-free bacon

1 tbsp (12 g) ghee

½ onion, diced

1 lb (454 g) ground chicken (see Cooking Tip)

1 tsp garlic powder

½ tsp sea salt

½ tsp paprika

3 cups (273 g) chopped (small) broccoli florets

¼ cup (60 ml) chicken broth

1 (16-oz [454-g]) bag frozen cauliflower rice

2 large eggs

1 cup (240 ml) dairy-free ranch dressing

Set the oven to 400°F (200°C)—no need to preheat. Line a rimmed baking sheet with foil or parchment paper

Lay the bacon pieces out flat on the baking sheet and cook for 12 to 15 minutes, or until crispy. When the bacon is done, remove the pan from the oven and drain the bacon on a paper towel-lined plate, and then crumble the bacon.

While the bacon is cooking, heat the ghee in a large skillet over medium heat. Add the onion and ground chicken. Cook for 4 to 5 minutes, or until the chicken is mostly browned, using a wooden spoon to break up the chicken. Add the garlic powder, salt and paprika and stir. Add the broccoli and the chicken broth and cover. Let it steam for 1 to 2 minutes, or until the broccoli turns bright green.

Add the frozen cauliflower rice to a 9 x 13-inch (23 x 33-cm) casserole dish, along with the chicken-broccoli mixture.

In a medium bowl, mix the eggs and ranch dressing, and then pour it over everything in the casserole dish. Mix everything well and use a spatula to smooth it out. Bake for 30 minutes. Top the casserole with bacon crumbles and serve.

Cooking Tip: *To use rotisserie or pre-cooked and shredded chicken, simply omit the chicken from the sauté steps. Heat the ghee in a sauté pan and cook the onion for 4 to 5 minutes. Add the garlic powder, salt, paprika, broccoli florets and chicken broth. Cover and let it steam for 1 to 2 minutes. Add the frozen cauliflower rice, 3 cups (375 g) pre-cooked shredded chicken, onion and broccoli mixture and ranch mixture to the casserole dish and stir to combine.*

"Cheese"-Burger Casserole

Egg-Free Option, Nut-Free Option

After sampling this casserole, my husband said it tasted just like a Big Mac, which is exactly what I was going for! I wanted to recreate all of the flavors of a big, juicy bacon cheeseburger in casserole form, but without any of the dairy or gluten. Mission accomplished . . . and it's seriously addicting! I used Kite Hill brand almond milk cream cheese as the dairy replacement, which can be found in many grocery stores. Frozen hash browns make up the bottom layer, which forms a nice mashed-potato consistency after baking. Save time by making the bacon ahead of time.

Yield: *4–6 servings*
Hands-On Time: *15 minutes*
Hands-Off Time: *30 minutes*

Avocado or olive oil cooking spray

6 pieces sugar-free bacon

1 lb (454 g) ground beef

½ medium onion, diced

2 cloves garlic, minced

¼ cup (60 ml) ketchup

2 tbsp (30 ml) yellow mustard

1 tbsp (15 ml) coconut aminos

1 tsp sea salt, plus extra as needed

4 oz (113 g) almond milk cream cheese (I like Kite Hill brand, see Cooking Tips)

1 (1-lb [454-g]) package frozen hash browns

3 eggs (see Cooking Tips)

½ tsp paprika (see Cooking Tips)

1 tbsp (15 ml) mayonnaise (see Cooking Tips)

Diced tomatoes, for serving (optional)

Shredded lettuce, for serving (optional)

Pickles, for serving (optional)

Set the oven to 400°F (200°C)—no need to preheat. Line a rimmed baking sheet with foil or parchment paper. Lightly spray a 9 x 13-inch (23 x 33-cm) casserole dish with the avocado or olive oil.

Lay the bacon pieces out flat on the baking sheet and cook for 12 to 15 minutes, or until crispy. When the bacon is done, remove the pan from the oven and drain the bacon on a paper towel–lined plate.

While the bacon is cooking, heat a large skillet over medium heat. Add the ground beef, onion and garlic. Cook for 4 to 5 minutes, stirring constantly while breaking up the meat, until mostly browned. Add the ketchup, mustard, coconut aminos, salt and cream cheese and stir until combined.

Place the frozen hash browns in the bottom of the casserole dish. Add the ground beef mixture on top of the hash browns and use a spatula to spread it out evenly.

In a small bowl, beat the eggs, paprika and mayonnaise together. Pour this mixture over the top of the ground beef mixture, and use a fork to lightly mix it into the top. Break the bacon into pieces, and add them to the top of the casserole, pressing down slightly.

Turn the oven down to 375°F (190°C). Bake the casserole for 30 minutes, or until the top is browned. Add your desired toppings.

Cooking Tips: *To make this nut free, omit the almond milk cream cheese and replace with 1 tablespoon (5 g) of nutritional yeast.*

To make this egg free, simply omit the egg, paprika and mayonnaise mixture. It will still taste delicious, although it may not hold together as well.

Jalapeño Tuna "Noodle" Casserole

Egg Free

I grew up eating the traditional version of this classic comfort food casserole made with pasta, peas and cream of mushroom soup. This healthier version has all of the flavors without any of the gluten, dairy, grains or MSG! It's made with spaghetti squash and a creamy coconut-cashew-mushroom sauce that tastes exactly like homemade cream of mushroom soup. There are a few different moving parts required for the hands-on time in this recipe, but it can all be done within 15 minutes if you are comfortable multitasking and working quickly. You start by cooking the squash in the oven while simultaneously making the filling and sauce. Sit back and relax while the squash finishes cooking, and then combine everything, top with some Paleo crackers and bake it! This may be a better recipe for a day when you have a little more time, but you can certainly make it faster by cooking the spaghetti squash the night before.

Yield: *4-6 servings*
Hands-On Time: *15 minutes*
Hands-Off Time: *35 minutes*

Avocado or olive oil cooking spray

1 (4-5-lb [1.8-2.3-kg]) spaghetti squash

1 tbsp (15 ml) olive oil

8 oz (226 g) white mushrooms, sliced

1 jalapeño, deseeded and sliced

2 cloves garlic, minced

½ cup (73 g) raw, unsalted cashews

½ cup (120 ml) full-fat coconut milk (stir well before measuring)

½ cup (120 ml) water

1 tbsp (15 ml) lemon juice

1 tsp onion powder

½ tsp paprika

1 tsp sea salt

1 tbsp (15 ml) sherry cooking wine

1¼ cups (300 ml) chicken broth

3 (5-oz [142-g]) cans tuna, drained

1 cup (56 g) crushed Paleo crackers or chips (I like Simple Mills and Siete Foods brands)

Preheat the oven to 400°F (200°C). Line a baking sheet with parchment paper. Lightly spray a 9 x 13-inch (23 x 33-cm) casserole dish with the avocado or olive oil.

Cut the spaghetti squash in half and scoop out the seeds. Place the halves cut side down on the baking sheet. Roast for 35 minutes.

While the squash is cooking, heat the olive oil in a large skillet over medium heat. Add the mushrooms, jalapeño and garlic. Cook for 5 minutes, stirring occasionally, until softened.

While the mushrooms cook, add the cashews, coconut milk, water, lemon juice, onion powder, paprika and salt to a high-speed blender. Blend on high for 1 minute, or until the sauce is very thick and creamy.

Add the sherry to the pan with the mushrooms and use a spoon to scrape up any brown bits from the bottom of the pan. Add the chicken broth and cashew cream, and bring it to a boil. Whisk for 1 to 2 minutes, or until the sauce is thickened. Stir in the tuna.

When the squash is done cooking, lower the oven temperature to 375°F (190°C). Scoop out the cooked spaghetti squash and add it to the casserole dish along with the tuna and mushroom mixture. Toss everything to combine. Top it with the crushed Paleo crackers or chips and bake for 25 to 30 minutes, or until it's cooked through and the edges are bubbling.

Cooking Tip: *If you do not have a high-speed blender like a Vitamix, I recommend soaking the cashews for at least 1 hour and then draining them before blending.*

Kick-Start the Day
Breakfast and Brunch

Breakfast is the most important meal of the day, and it also happens to be my favorite. Gone are the days where I would skip breakfast and chug a sugar-filled latte, only to be starving by 9 a.m. It can feel challenging to find breakfast options when you are eliminating gluten, grains and dairy; however, this chapter is packed with sweet and savory ideas that will leave you feeling satisfied and ready to take on the day!

This section also has a bunch of options that can be made ahead of time and reheated for a quick and easy breakfast on the go. Some of my favorites include the Buffalo Chicken Breakfast Casserole (page 141), Sausage, Spinach and Mushroom Frittata (page 145), Make-Ahead Sausage and Pepper Breakfast Bowls (page 150) and Pepperoni Pizza Egg Cups (page 154).

The Sweet Potato-Apple Breakfast Custard (page 137) and Strawberry-Rhubarb Chia Pudding (page 149) are sweeter options that do not need to be reheated, so you can simply take them out of the refrigerator and be on your way.

I think it's also important to remember that you can eat these types of meals any time of day—it doesn't have to just be for breakfast. All of these would also make a delicious lunch, dinner or snack!

BLT Breakfast Scramble

Low Carb, Nut Free, Vegetarian Option

Egg scrambles are one of my go-to breakfasts on busy weekday mornings. They only take a few minutes to prepare, and the possibilities are endless when it comes to the meats and veggies you can add. This scramble has the classic combo of bacon, "lettuce" (spinach) and tomato topped with some avocado for extra-healthy fats. The eggs get cooked directly in the rendered bacon fat, which gives this dish incredible flavor. Cook the bacon ahead of time and store it in the refrigerator to save time.

Yield: *2 servings*
Hands–On Time: *10 minutes*
Hands–Off Time: *none*

4 pieces sugar-free bacon (see Cooking Tip)

4 large eggs

1 small tomato, diced fine

½ avocado, peeled and sliced

2 handfuls raw spinach

¼ tsp sea salt

Black pepper, to taste

Everything bagel seasoning (I like Trader Joe's Everything But the Bagel seasoning, optional)

Cut the bacon into 1-inch (2.5-cm) pieces. Heat a skillet over medium heat and add the bacon pieces. Cook for 5 to 7 minutes, stirring occasionally, or until cooked through and crispy.

While the bacon is cooking, beat the eggs in a small bowl. Dice the tomatoes and slice the avocado. When the bacon is crispy, add the spinach and tomatoes to the skillet. Stir until the spinach begins to wilt, about 1 minute. Add the eggs and the salt and pepper, and stir until the eggs are cooked through and everything is combined. Top with the avocado slices and everything bagel seasoning, if desired.

Cooking Tip: *To make this vegetarian, omit the bacon. You can also use ham instead of bacon. Simply use ghee as the cooking fat instead of the bacon fat.*

Sweet Potato-Apple Breakfast Custard

Nut-Free Option, Vegetarian

The texture of this casserole reminds me of bread pudding or the filling from a pumpkin or sweet potato pie. It is a nice way to switch things up if you're looking for something on the sweeter side, or if you're just getting tired of eggs! It is delicious served warm or chilled, and it pairs perfectly with a hot cup of coffee.

Yield: *6–8 servings*
Hands-On Time: *10 minutes*
Hands-Off Time: *35–40 minutes*

1 tbsp (15 g) coconut oil

1 small apple (any type), peeled, cored and diced (see Cooking Tips)

½ tsp cinnamon

4 eggs

1 (15-oz [424-g]) can sweet potato puree (see Cooking Tips)

1 cup (240 ml) full-fat coconut milk (stir well before measuring)

2 ripe bananas

2 tbsp (30 ml) maple syrup (see Cooking Tips)

1 tsp vanilla extract

1 tsp pumpkin pie spice

¼ tsp sea salt

½ cup (55 g) chopped pecans (see Cooking Tips)

Preheat the oven to 325°F (165°C).

Heat the coconut oil in a sauté pan and add the apple and cinnamon. Sauté for 3 to 4 minutes, or until the apple begins to soften. Set the apple aside.

In a 9 x 13-inch (23 x 33-cm) casserole dish, combine the eggs, sweet potato puree, coconut milk, bananas, maple syrup, vanilla, pumpkin pie spice and salt. Mix using an immersion blender or electric hand mixer until everything is well combined. Add the cinnamon-coated apples and fold them into the mixture. Sprinkle the pecans evenly over the top of the sweet potato and apple mixture. Bake for 35 to 40 minutes, or until the top is set. Let it cool, and then cut into slices. This will stay fresh in the refrigerator for up to 4 days.

Cooking Tips: *You can omit the apple for more of a smooth custard.*

You can substitute pumpkin puree for the sweet potato puree, if you prefer.

Omit the maple syrup to make this sugar free.

To make this nut free, omit the pecans.

Sausage Gravy Hash Brown Casserole

Egg-Free Option, Nut Free

Sausage and gravy is a classic Southern comfort food and used to be a must-have whenever I went to Cracker Barrel for breakfast. Unfortunately, it's not the healthiest meal, so I decided to create a Paleo version using coconut milk and tapioca starch instead of flour and milk. The sausage and gravy gets baked with hash browns to make the perfect egg-free breakfast casserole. It's also delicious served with a runny egg on top! You could also serve it with a side of fruit or roasted vegetables instead of eggs.

Yield: *4–6 servings*
Hands–On Time: *15 minutes*
Hands–Off Time: *25 minutes*

Avocado or olive oil cooking spray

1 tbsp (15 ml) olive oil

1 lb (454 g) sugar-free pork sausage

1½ tbsp (7 g) tapioca starch

1 (13.5-oz [398-ml]) can coconut milk (stir well before pouring)

1 tsp dried sage

½ tsp garlic powder

½ tsp onion powder

½ tsp dried thyme

½ tsp sea salt

1 lb (454 g) frozen hash browns

Fried eggs, for serving (optional)

Preheat the oven to 375°F (190°C). Spray a 9 x 13-inch (23 x 33-cm) casserole dish with the avocado or olive oil.

Heat the olive oil in a large skillet over medium heat and add the sausage. Break it up using a wooden spoon and cook for 5 to 7 minutes, or until mostly browned. Do not drain the fat. Add the tapioca starch and stir until it's no longer lumpy and it begins to bubble. Add the coconut milk and stir. Bring to a boil, and then reduce the heat and simmer while stirring for 1 to 2 minutes, or until thickened. Add the sage, garlic powder, onion powder, thyme and salt and stir. Turn the heat to low.

Spread the frozen hash browns out in an even layer in the bottom of the casserole dish. Add the sausage gravy mixture on top, using a spatula to spread it out evenly. Bake the casserole for 25 minutes, or until the hash browns are cooked through and the casserole is crispy around the edges. Serve the casserole topped with a fried egg or two, if desired.

Buffalo Chicken Breakfast Casserole

Low Carb, Nut Free

Buffalo chicken will forever be one of my favorite dishes. In this casserole, pre-cooked shredded chicken gets combined with eggs, green onions, hot sauce, mayo and spices to create a delicious breakfast bake. This is perfect for feeding a crowd and also for making on a Sunday to heat up for quick breakfasts throughout the week. I've also included options below for how to quickly make pulled chicken if you don't have pre-cooked or rotisserie chicken on hand!

Yield: *6-8 servings*
Hands-On Time: *10 minutes*
Hands-Off Time: *35-40 minutes*

Ghee or cooking oil

12 eggs

¼ cup (60 ml) almond milk or full-fat coconut milk

¼ cup (60 ml) mayonnaise

½ cup (120 ml) buffalo or hot sauce (I like Frank's RedHot)

2 cups (250 g) pre-cooked, shredded chicken (see Cooking Tips)

¼ cup (12 g) diced green onions, plus more for garnish

1 tsp garlic powder

1 tsp onion powder

½ tsp paprika

½ tsp sea salt

2 tsp (1 g) chopped fresh dill or 1 tsp dried

Dairy-free ranch dressing (I like Tessamae's), for serving

Preheat the oven to 375°F (190°C). Lightly grease a 9 x 13-inch (23 x 33-cm) casserole dish with ghee or cooking oil.

Add the eggs to a large bowl and beat well. Add the almond milk, mayonnaise and buffalo sauce. Stir well to combine. Add the chicken, green onions, garlic powder, onion powder, paprika, salt and dill, and stir. Pour the mixture into the casserole dish. Bake for 35 to 40 minutes, or until the center is set and the eggs are no longer runny. Top with your favorite dairy-free ranch dressing and more green onions and serve. This casserole can be stored in the refrigerator for up to 3 to 4 days.

Cooking Tips: *If you are using a rotisserie chicken, be sure to check your ingredients. Many contain sugar and other additives that are not Paleo-friendly.*

If you do not have pre-cooked chicken available and would like to make your own, you can quickly poach some using this method: Add 2 chicken breasts to a large pot of water and bring it to a boil. Once boiling, cover and remove from the heat. Let the pot sit for 15 minutes, and then drain and shred the chicken.

Bananas Foster-Stuffed Sweet Potatoes

Egg Free, Nut-Free Option, Vegan Option

Traditional bananas Foster is made with cinnamon, sugar, dark rum and banana liquor and then lit on fire. In this alcohol-free (and fire-free) breakfast version, the bananas are caramelized with pecans in a sauce made from ghee and maple syrup and then stuffed into sweet potatoes. This makes a great egg-free breakfast, or even a healthier dessert option! To save time, you can make the sweet potatoes the night before and reheat them when ready to serve with the bananas.

Yield: *3 stuffed potatoes*

Hands-On Time: *5 minutes*

Hands-Off Time: *45 minutes (if cooking sweet potatoes in the oven)*

3 medium sweet potatoes

¼ cup (48 g) ghee (see Cooking Tips)

⅓ cup (80 ml) maple syrup

1 tsp vanilla extract

½ tsp cinnamon

3 medium ripe bananas, sliced into rounds

¼ cup (27 g) chopped pecans (see Cooking Tips)

1 tbsp (6 g) shredded coconut, for serving

Poke holes in the potatoes with a fork. You can either cook the potatoes in the microwave for 5 to 7 minutes, or roast them in the oven at 425°F (220°C) for 45 minutes.

Melt the ghee in a large skillet over medium heat. Add the maple syrup, vanilla and cinnamon, and stir until it bubbles. Add the bananas and pecans and cook for 2 to 3 minutes, or until they are coated and softened. Serve the caramelized bananas and pecans in the cooked sweet potatoes and top with the coconut shreds.

Cooking Tips: *To make this vegan, replace the ghee with coconut oil.*

To make this nut free, omit the pecans.

Sausage, Spinach and Mushroom Frittata

Low Carb, Nut Free

I love making frittatas on a Sunday morning and having a bunch of leftovers to heat up throughout the week. This simple recipe only has five main ingredients, and it's all made in one pan. Fewer dishes = happy mama! I also like adding spinach and/or kale to my egg dishes to sneak in some extra veggies, but you can truly customize this frittata using whatever protein and veggies you have on hand. Any type of dairy-free milk will work as well.

Yield: *6–8 slices*
Hands-On Time: *10 minutes*
Hands-Off Time: *15 minutes*

1 tbsp (15 ml) olive oil or avocado oil

16 oz (454 g) sugar-free breakfast or Italian sausage

8 oz (226 g) cremini mushrooms, chopped

10 eggs

¼ cup (60 ml) almond milk or full-fat coconut milk

2 tsp (6 g) everything bagel seasoning (I like Trader Joe's Everything But the Bagel)

¼ tsp sea salt

2 cups (60 g) raw spinach

Dairy-free ranch dressing and/or hot sauce, for serving (optional)

Preheat the oven to 375°F (190°C).

Heat the oil in a cast-iron or other oven-safe skillet over medium heat. Add the sausage and mushrooms, and cook for 5 to 7 minutes, or until the sausage is browned and cooked through. Use a wooden spoon to break it up into pieces. While the sausage and mushrooms are cooking, in a large bowl, whisk the eggs, non-dairy milk, bagel seasoning and salt.

Add the spinach to the pan with the sausage and mushrooms and stir for 1 to 2 minutes, until it's wilted. Pour the egg mixture over the sausage mixture, using a spatula to spread it out evenly. Bake for 15 minutes, or until the eggs are set. Slice and serve with dairy-free ranch dressing and/or hot sauce if you'd like! This frittata can be cut up and stored in the refrigerator for up to 4 days.

Mexican Breakfast Lasagna

Nut-Free Option, Vegetarian Option

This unique breakfast casserole has layers of Paleo tortillas, chorizo (which is a spicy Mexican sausage), salsa and eggs. It's delicious topped with avocado and cilantro. To meal prep and save time, you can make the layers ahead of time and pour the egg mixture over the top whenever you're ready to bake it! I love this casserole because it uses minimal ingredients, but it is packed with flavor in every bite.

Yield: *6-8 servings*
Hands-On Time: *10 minutes*
Hands-Off Time: *35-40 minutes*

Avocado or olive oil cooking spray

1 lb (454 g) chorizo (ground or removed from casing, see Cooking Tips)

12 eggs

1 tsp chili powder

1 tsp cumin

1 tsp garlic powder

½ tsp paprika

½ tsp sea salt

8 Paleo tortillas (I like Siete Foods brand, see Cooking Tips)

1 (16-oz [454-g]) jar salsa

Sliced avocado, for serving (optional)

Fresh cilantro, for serving (optional)

Preheat the oven to 375°F (190°C). Spray a 9 x 13-inch (23 x 33-cm) casserole dish with the avocado or olive oil.

Heat a large skillet over medium heat and add the chorizo. Cook for 5 to 7 minutes, or until mostly browned and cooked through. While the chorizo is cooking, in a large bowl, beat the eggs with the chili powder, cumin, garlic powder, paprika and sea salt.

Place 4 of the tortillas on the bottom of the casserole dish to cover it, overlapping if necessary. Spoon half of the chorizo on top of the tortillas, and then spoon half of the jar of salsa on top of the chorizo. Repeat this step with 4 more tortillas, the rest of the chorizo and the rest of the salsa. Pour the egg and spice mixture over the entire casserole as evenly as possible. Use a fork to even it out and slightly mix the eggs into the chorizo and salsa on top. Bake for 35 to 40 minutes, or until the eggs are set and the edges are browned. Serve with avocado and cilantro, if desired. This casserole can be stored in the refrigerator for up to 4 days.

Cooking Tips: *Look for chorizo without sugar, if possible, to keep this meal Paleo. Omit it for a vegetarian meal.*

Siete Foods makes a cassava Paleo tortilla. Use these for a nut-free recipe. They also have almond flour tortillas.

Strawberry-Rhubarb Chia Pudding

Egg Free, Nut Free, Vegan

I'm usually more of a savory breakfast kinda gal, but every now and then it's nice to switch it up to something sweet! Chia pudding is a delicious, plant-based meal that is packed with fiber and antioxidants. This recipe comes together quickly, and you can change up the fruit, nut and flavor additions using whatever you have on hand. For this recipe, we top the chia pudding with a strawberry-rhubarb compote that is made on the stove in just 5 minutes. These pudding cups keep well in the refrigerator, so they are perfect for meal prep!

Yield: *4 cups*
Hands-On Time: *10 minutes*
Hands-Off Time: *5 minutes*

1 (13.5-oz [398-ml]) can full-fat coconut milk (stir well before pouring)

½ cup (81 g) chia seeds

2 tbsp (30 ml) maple syrup, divided

½ tsp vanilla extract

1 cup (144 g) frozen or fresh strawberries

1 cup (122 g) frozen sliced rhubarb (see Cooking Tips)

2 tbsp (30 ml) water

Mix the coconut milk, chia seeds, 1 tablespoon (15 ml) of the maple syrup and vanilla in a bowl. Set it aside so the chia pudding can form.

Add the strawberries, rhubarb, remaining maple syrup and water to a saucepan, and bring to a boil. Once boiling, reduce the heat to medium. Use a potato masher to mash up the fruit while it cooks for 3 to 4 minutes. Turn off the heat and let it cool for a few minutes.

Fill each serving jar halfway with the chia seed pudding, and then top with the strawberry-rhubarb compote. Eat immediately, or for best results, cover and place in the refrigerator for 1 to 2 hours. These pudding cups can be stored in the refrigerator for up to 4 days.

Cooking Tips: *Frozen sliced rhubarb can be found in the freezer section of many stores. I use Dole brand.*

I love to use Weck Mini Tulip Jelly Jars for this recipe. They are the perfect size and hold up to 8 ounces (237 ml).

Make-Ahead Sausage and Pepper Breakfast Bowls

Egg-Free Option, Low Carb, Nut Free

Meal prepping for the week ahead is one of the best things you can do to stay on track. As my dad always said, "Fail to plan, plan to fail." This easy sheet-pan meal is ready in less than 30 minutes and is perfect for making ahead and taking with you on busy mornings! It's delicious on its own for an egg-free option, or you can serve with eggs and avocado. It would also make a great filling for easy breakfast tacos.

Yield: *3-4 servings*
Hands-On Time: *10 minutes*
Hands-Off Time: *25 minutes*

1 (14-oz [397-g]) package smoked sausage or kielbasa, cut into ¼-inch (6-mm) rounds (I like Pederson's Farms brand)

½ medium onion, cut into 1-inch (2.5-cm) pieces

1 red bell pepper, cut into 2-inch (5-cm) slices

1 yellow bell pepper, cut into 2-inch (5-cm) slices

1 tbsp (15 ml) olive oil

1 tbsp (15 ml) coconut aminos

½ tsp paprika

½ tsp sea salt

Eggs, for serving (optional)

Avocado, for serving (optional)

Taco shells, for serving (optional)

Preheat the oven to 425°F (220°C). Line a rimmed baking sheet with parchment paper for easy cleanup.

Place the sausage rounds, onion and bell peppers in a bowl and toss with the olive oil, coconut aminos, paprika and salt. Spread everything out evenly on the baking sheet, making sure they don't overlap too much. Bake for 25 minutes, flipping at the 15-minute mark. Serve as is, with eggs and avocado, if desired, or in tacos. This dish will stay good in the refrigerator for up to 4 days.

Eggless Breakfast Hash

Egg Free, Nut Free, Vegan Option

I personally never tire of eggs, but I know a lot of people that do! It can be tricky to think of what to eat for breakfast (other than eggs) when you are avoiding grains and dairy. This skillet chicken sausage, sweet potato and kale hash is delicious with some ranch dressing and added avocado for some healthy fats. You can definitely add eggs to it as well. You can also use whatever veggies, potatoes or sausage you have on hand.

Yield: *3-4 servings*

Hands-On Time: *10 minutes*

Hands-Off Time: *10 minutes*

1 tbsp (15 ml) olive oil or avocado oil, plus more if needed

1 (12-oz [340-g]) package chicken sausage (I used 6 sausages), cut into rounds (see Cooking Tips)

3 cups (402 g) cubed sweet potatoes or 1 (1-lb [454-g]) package pre-cut sweet potatoes

4 cups (268 g) coarsely chopped kale, stems removed

½ tsp garlic powder

½ tsp paprika

½ tsp sea salt

¼ cup (60 ml) chicken broth (see Cooking Tips)

Avocado slices, for serving (optional)

Heat the oil in a cast-iron skillet over medium heat. Add the sausage rounds and cook for 2 minutes on each side. Add the sweet potatoes and stir. Cover the pan and cook for 5 minutes. Stir the potatoes and sausage and add more oil (or lower the heat) if you notice it starting to burn or stick. Cook for 5 minutes. Add the kale, garlic powder, paprika, salt and chicken broth. Stir everything together for 1 to 2 minutes, or until the kale is wilted and the liquid has cooked off. Serve with a side of avocado.

Cooking Tips: *To keep this vegan, omit the sausage and use vegetable broth instead of chicken broth. Other vegetable ideas to add include butternut squash, spinach and mushrooms.*

Pepperoni Pizza Egg Cups

Low Carb, Nut Free, Vegetarian Option

Egg cups are a great way to meal prep for the week with only 10 minutes of actual prep time! I love making a batch on a Sunday and reheating a couple for an easy breakfast throughout the week. I gave these egg cups a pizza theme with green bell peppers, mushrooms, marinara sauce, Italian seasoning and pepperoni, but you can certainly customize them using whatever you have on hand!

Yield: *12 egg cups*
Prep time: *10 minutes*
Cook time: *20 minutes*

Avocado or olive oil cooking spray

½ cup (75 g) diced green bell pepper

½ cup (35 g) diced mushrooms

¼ cup (60 ml) sugar-free marinara sauce (I like Rao's Homemade brand)

10 eggs

½ tsp sea salt

1 tsp Italian seasoning

12 slices uncured and sugar-free pepperoni (see Cooking Tip)

Dairy-free ranch dressing, for serving

Preheat the oven to 375°F (190°C). Spray a muffin pan with the avocado or olive oil. I've found that silicone muffin pans work best when it comes to helping the eggs not stick to the pan.

Add about ½ tablespoon (5 g) of the diced bell pepper and mushrooms to each cup. Spoon 1 teaspoon of marinara sauce into each cup. Set aside.

Add the eggs and salt to a bowl and beat well. Pour the egg mixture evenly into each cup, filling them about two-thirds of the way to the top. I like to use a large measuring cup with a spout to make for easier and cleaner pouring. Sprinkle each cup with some of the Italian seasoning, and top each one with a pepperoni slice.

Bake for 22 to 23 minutes, or until the eggs are fully set and no longer runny. Let them cool, and then pop out of the cups and serve with Paleo-friendly ranch dressing.

You can store these egg cups in an airtight container or plastic bag for up to 4 days in the refrigerator. To reheat, simply microwave for 30 to 45 seconds, or pop into the oven at 350°F (180°C) for 10 minutes, or until heated through.

Cooking Tip: *To make these vegetarian, omit the pepperoni.*

Staple
Side Dishes

All of the side dishes in this chapter can be prepped in 10 minutes or less, so you can create delicious accompaniments for your main meal without much time or effort. These recipes are also a great way to get more vegetables into your diet, and there is something for everyone: low-carb, vegan, egg-free and nut-free options.

These family-friendly side dishes are classics made with minimal ingredients and a Paleo twist. I've included techniques for roasting vegetables so they are never overcooked or mushy (see Perfect Roasted Spaghetti Squash [page 169]) and also tips for how to save time in the kitchen.

Some favorites from this section include Orange Curried Carrots and Parsnips (page 166), Spicy Roasted Broccolini (page 165) and Garlic Cauliflower Mash (page 162).

Sweet and Spicy Oven-Baked Sweet Potato Fries

Egg Free, Nut Free, Vegan

Sweet potato fries have become a staple in my household. They go well with burgers, salads, Easy Instant Pot Pulled BBQ Chicken (page 73) and so many other dishes. They also make an excellent breakfast! This simple oven-baked recipe includes a bit of cinnamon and cayenne pepper, which gives these fries their sweet and spicy flavors. I love dipping these into ketchup or almond butter! To make these into regular sweet potato fries, omit the cayenne pepper and cinnamon. This recipe also works well with parsnips that have been peeled and sliced into fry shapes. Save time by cutting your fries ahead of time and storing them in a tightly sealed contained in the refrigerator for up to 2 days ahead of time.

Yield: *3-4 servings*
Hands-On Time: *5 minutes*
Hands-Off Time: *35 minutes*

2 large sweet potatoes, scrubbed

1 tbsp (15 ml) olive oil or avocado oil

½ tsp cinnamon

½ tsp sea salt

¼ tsp cayenne pepper

Ketchup, for serving (optional)

Preheat the oven to 425°F (220°C) and line a rimmed baking sheet with parchment paper or foil.

Cut the potatoes into fries by first slicing off the ends and then cutting each potato in half horizontally. Cut the halves into 4 pieces one way, and then the other. This will create fries that are approximately 3 inches (8 cm) long and ¼ to ½ inch (6 mm to 1.3 cm) thick.

Place the fries into a bowl with the oil, cinnamon, salt and cayenne pepper, and toss to combine. Spread the coated fries out evenly on the baking sheet, making sure they are not overlapping and have enough room. This will help them to get crisp. Bake for 30 minutes. Check them at the 15-minute mark to ensure they aren't getting too browned. If they are, you can flip them. Broil for an additional 5 minutes to get them extra browned and crispy. Serve with a side of ketchup, if desired.

Lemony Green Beans with Toasted Almonds

Egg Free, Low Carb, Nut-Free Option, Vegan Option

This version of classic green beans almondine is taken to the next level with some fresh lemon juice, lemon zest, garlic and shallots. It is packed with flavor, very simple to make and can be made very quickly. I like to pair this recipe with my Perfect Dutch Oven Roasted Chicken (page 89), Creamy Salmon Piccata (page 37) and Slow Cooker Smothered Pork Chops (page 50).

Yield: *4-5 servings*
Hands-On Time: *10 minutes*
Hands-Off Time: *5 minutes*

1 lb (454 g) green beans, ends trimmed

½ cup (54 g) thinly sliced almonds (see Cooking Tips)

2 tbsp (24 g) ghee (see Cooking Tips)

1 shallot, peeled and diced

2 cloves garlic, minced

1 tbsp (15 ml) lemon juice

1 tsp lemon zest

½ tsp sea salt

¼ tsp black pepper

Bring a large pot of water to a boil. Add the green beans and cook for 4 to 5 minutes, or until crisp tender. Transfer the beans to an ice bath to halt the cooking.

While the beans are cooking, heat a large skillet over medium heat. Add the almonds and dry toast them for 1 to 2 minutes. Remove them and set aside on a plate.

Add the ghee to the pan. When it's melted, add the diced shallot and garlic. Cook for 2 to 3 minutes until they begin to soften. Add the green beans to the pan along with the lemon juice, lemon zest and toasted almonds. Toss everything to combine. Sprinkle the green beans with the salt and pepper and serve.

Cooking Tips: *To make this nut free, omit the almonds.*
To make this vegan, use coconut oil or olive oil instead of ghee.

Garlic Cauliflower Mash

Egg Free, Low Carb, Nut-Free Option, Vegan Option

If you don't love potatoes or are looking to keep things low carb, mashed cauliflower is a perfect side dish! It truly has the consistency of mashed potatoes, and the garlicky, buttery flavors in this dish are the perfect accompaniment to so many meals. I use pre-minced garlic to save time, and I use ghee instead of regular butter to keep it Paleo. I love serving this with Slow Cooker Smothered Pork Chops (page 50) and Cottage Pie Bowls (page 38).

Yield: *3–4 servings*
Hands–On Time: *5 minutes*
Hands–Off Time: *15 minutes*

1 large head cauliflower, chopped into large florets

2 cloves garlic, minced

2 tbsp (24 g) ghee (see Cooking Tips)

1½ tsp (9 g) sea salt, plus more to taste

¼ cup (60 ml) full-fat coconut milk (stir well before measuring) or almond milk (see Cooking Tips)

Black pepper, to taste

Bring a large pot of water to a boil. Add the cauliflower florets and cover. Cook for about 15 minutes, or until fork-tender. Drain the cauliflower and return it to the pot. Add the garlic, ghee, salt and non-dairy milk. Use an immersion blender to achieve ultimate creaminess. Alternatively, you can use a regular hand masher. Add salt and pepper to taste and serve with your favorite protein!

Cooking Tips: *To make this vegan, use olive oil instead of ghee.*

Don't use almond milk if you want to keep this recipe nut free.

Simple Classic Coleslaw

Low Carb, Nut Free, Vegetarian

A summer BBQ isn't complete without a delicious creamy coleslaw! I absolutely love this four-ingredient version, which has no dairy, gluten or refined sugar. A bit of maple syrup gives it the perfect amount of sweetness. I like to use a bag of pre-cut coleslaw mix to save time.

Yield: *3-4 servings*
Hands-On Time: *5 minutes*
Hands-Off Time: *none*

1 (14-oz [397-g]) bag coleslaw mix
1 tbsp (15 ml) apple cider vinegar
¼ cup (60 ml) mayonnaise
½ tbsp (8 ml) maple syrup

Combine the coleslaw mix, apple cider vinegar, mayonnaise and maple syrup in a large bowl and mix well. Refrigerate until you're ready to serve. Store this coleslaw in the refrigerator for up to 3 to 5 days.

Spicy Roasted Broccolini

Egg Free, Low Carb, Nut Free, Vegan

Broccolini, or baby broccoli, is one of my favorite side dishes to prepare. It has a delicious crunch and pairs well with so many different recipes. I like to massage the oil into the tops of the broccolini to ensure it is packed with flavor and crispiness! The crushed red pepper is optional but gives this broccolini the perfect amount of heat.

Yield: *3-4 servings*
Hands-On Time: *5 minutes*
Hands-Off Time: *11-12 minutes*

1 lb (454 g) broccolini
2 tbsp (30 ml) olive oil
1 clove garlic, minced
Crushed red pepper flakes, to taste
1 tbsp (15 ml) lemon juice
½ tsp sea salt
¼ tsp black pepper

Preheat the oven to 425°F (220°C). Line a rimmed baking sheet with parchment paper or a baking mat. In a large bowl, combine the broccolini, olive oil, garlic, crushed red pepper flakes and lemon juice. Mix well using your hands. Spread the broccolini out evenly on the baking sheet and sprinkle with the salt and pepper. Roast for 11 to 12 minutes, or until the broccolini is crispy and bright green. Serve with your favorite main dish.

* See image on page 156.

Orange Curried Carrots and Parsnips

Egg Free, Nut Free, Vegetarian

My mom has always made a rendition of these orange curried carrots and parsnips for Thanksgiving every year, and they are so incredibly delicious. I knew I needed to recreate them Paleo style! The carrots and parsnips are roasted with ghee and salt, and then we add a glaze made from freshly squeezed orange juice, orange zest, curry powder and honey. The mixture caramelizes in the oven and creates the most incredible flavors. This dish truly tastes like candy! This side dish is delicious with the Chicken Cordon Bleu Bake (page 122), Slow Cooker Smothered Pork Chops (page 50) and the Better-For-You Mississippi Pot Roast (page 70). To save time, peel and cut your carrots and parsnips up to 2 days ahead of time, and store them in a tightly sealed container in the refrigerator.

Yield: *4-6 servings*
Hands-On Time: *10 minutes*
Hands-Off Time: *30 minutes*

1 lb (454 g) carrots, peeled and sliced into ½-inch (1.3-cm)-thick pieces

1 lb (454 g) parsnips, peeled and sliced into ½-inch (1.3-cm)-thick pieces

2 tbsp (30 ml) melted ghee

½ tsp sea salt

½ tbsp (3 g) curry powder

¼ cup (60 ml) freshly squeezed orange juice

1 tsp orange zest

1 tbsp (15 ml) honey

Fresh parsley, for serving (optional)

Preheat the oven to 425°F (220°C).

Peel and slice the carrots and parsnips. Place them on a baking sheet, drizzle with the ghee and sprinkle with the salt. Toss everything to coat well. Bake for 15 minutes.

Combine the curry powder, orange juice, orange zest and honey in a small saucepan. Bring to a boil, whisk well and then remove the pan from the heat. Pour the glaze over the veggies, and use two spatulas to toss everything together. Roast for 15 minutes. Transfer the carrots and parsnips to a bowl and pour any remaining glaze on top. Serve with fresh parsley, if desired.

Perfect Roasted Spaghetti Squash

Egg Free, Nut Free, Vegan

Spaghetti squash noodles go perfectly with so many dishes. They are also delicious on their own with a bit of olive oil, salt and pepper. I like to cut the squash in half horizontally around the middle because it creates longer spaghetti-like strands. You can also cut it vertically to create boats; however, it may be harder to cut the squash open. I find that the method below creates the perfect spaghetti squash every time: never overcooked, mushy or watery! I like to serve this with my Quick Creamy Bolognese Sauce (page 93) and Slow Cooker Classic Italian Meatballs (page 58).

Yield: *3-4 servings*

Hands-On Time: *5 minutes*

Hands-Off Time: *30-40 minutes (depending on the size of your squash)*

1 large spaghetti squash (see Cooking Tip)

2 tsp (10 ml) olive oil

¼ tsp sea salt

Preheat the oven to 400°F (200°C). Line a baking sheet with parchment paper.

Cut the squash around the middle horizontally. Rub a bit of olive oil on each half and sprinkle with salt. Place each half cut side down on the baking sheet and bake for 30 to 40 minutes, or until fork-tender. Use a fork to scoop out the "spaghetti" strands.

Cooking Tip: *If you have a smaller squash, it may cook in as little as 30 minutes. If your squash is on the larger side, it may take 40 minutes. You'll know it is done when you can easily pierce the skin with a fork.*

"Cheesy" Mashed Potatoes

Egg Free, Nut-Free Option, Vegetarian, Vegan Option

Mashed potatoes are my all-time favorite side dish. This unique dairy-free version gets a delicious "cheesy" flavor from nutritional yeast and a creaminess from a combination of blended cashews and coconut milk. These mashed potatoes are the perfect accompaniment to Cottage Pie Bowls (page 38), Prosciutto, Chicken and Asparagus Bundles with Blistered Tomatoes (page 26) and Better-For-You Mississippi Pot Roast (page 70).

Yield: *3-4 servings*
Hands-On Time: *5 minutes*
Hands-Off Time: *20 minutes*

2½ lbs (1 kg) russet potatoes (about 3 large potatoes), peeled and cut into large chunks

½ cup (73 g) raw, unsalted cashews (see Cooking Tips)

½ cup (120 ml) full-fat coconut milk (stir well before measuring)

⅓ cup (80 ml) water (see Cooking Tips)

1 tbsp (15 ml) lemon juice (see Cooking Tips)

1 clove garlic, minced

2 tbsp (10 g) nutritional yeast (see Cooking Tips)

2 tbsp (28 g) ghee (or olive oil for a vegan option)

2 tsp (12 g) sea salt

¼ tsp paprika

Add the potato chunks to a large pot of water. Cover and bring it to a boil. Cook the potatoes for 15 minutes, or until fork-tender.

While the potatoes are cooking, add the cashews, coconut milk, water, lemon juice, garlic and nutritional yeast to a high-speed blender. Blend on high for 1 minute, or until very smooth and creamy.

Drain the potatoes and return them to the pot. Add the ghee, salt, paprika and cashew "cheese" sauce. Use a potato masher to mash everything together until your desired level of creaminess has been reached. Alternatively, you can use an immersion blender.

Cooking Tips: *To make these nut free, omit the cashews and the water. Do not blend the remaining ingredients (coconut milk, lemon juice, garlic and nutritional yeast); simply add them to the pot with the ghee, salt and paprika and mash it all together.*

To make regular mashed potatoes without the "cheesy" flavor, omit the nutritional yeast and lemon juice. Add the cashews, coconut milk, water and garlic to a blender and blend on high for 1 minute. Follow the remaining instructions.

If you do not have a high-speed blender like a Vitamix, I recommend soaking the cashews for at least 1 hour and then draining them before blending.

Acknowledgments

Thank you . . .

. . . to my kids, Annabel, Finn and Liam. Thank you for putting up with me as I navigated how to balance everything during the process of writing this book. There were good days and tough ones, but your hugs and sweet smiles kept me going through it all!

. . . to my husband, Bryan, for telling me to go for it when I wasn't sure if I was good enough to write a book, for always helping me eat the leftovers and for giving constructive criticism, even when I didn't want to hear it. For making the weekends fun for the kids when I had to spend time working and for (almost) never complaining about my constant frazzled state. And for always supporting my dreams, no matter how crazy they may be. Thanks for being our rock!

. . . to my mom, for always making the best homemade meals when I was growing up and for showing me that patience is a virtue. For always being willing to help and for being such a positive, loving and present figure in our lives. We love you!

. . . to my dad, for teaching me that hard work pays off and that you can do anything you put your mind to. For always reminding me to have a plan and work the plan. And for passing along your foodie gene . . . I think you may be the only person in my life who loves good food as much as I do!

. . . to Kiki, for all of your love and support! Thanks for being the best Smom a girl could ask for.

. . . to Tom, Parker and Bay. I feel so lucky to have some of the most creative, hilarious and smart human beings for siblings. Thank you for helping me with photography and marketing stuff and for always making me laugh. I love you!

. . . to Amy and Steve, for always believing in me and for being the best taste testers!

. . . to Kaht, Kimmy, Foley and Sal. I am so grateful for your lifelong friendships. Thank you for being my biggest cheerleaders, for helping me test recipes and for always making me smile! I love you guys so much.

. . . to my Amherst mamas. Thank you for being the village I never knew I needed, for helping with the kids, for taking extra food off my hands and for always being willing to have a glass of wine with me.

. . . to Sarah, Meg, Rosie and the entire Page Street Publishing team. Thank you for making my dream a reality. I appreciate all of your help and patience along the way. It's been an honor to work with you all!

. . . and to my Mary's Whole Life readers and community, THANK YOU. Without your support, none of this would be possible. I truly appreciate every comment, recipe rating, sweet message and word of encouragement. Knowing I'm helping even one person makes this all worth it. From the bottom of my heart, thank you! I love you all.

About the Author

Mary Smith is the creator, blogger and photographer behind Mary's Whole Life, a food and healthy living blog with delicious and easy gluten-free and Paleo recipes for the whole family.

After being diagnosed with celiac disease at age 33, Mary set out on a journey to figure out how to create delicious comfort food staples using real ingredients and without sacrificing taste. She believes in enjoying life to the fullest, and having a dietary restriction shouldn't have to limit that! Mary's recipes and work have been featured on the feedfeed, PopSugar, Parade.com, Prevention.com and more.

In addition to cooking, Mary enjoys traveling, completing DIY home projects, running and hanging out with her family. She has a bachelor's degree in public relations and a passion for helping other busy moms navigate how to eat healthy while balancing it all. She lives in Westminster, Maryland, with her husband, Bryan, and three kids, Annabel, Finn and Liam.

Index